How To Build
Network Marketing
LEADERS

VOLUME TWO

Activities and
Lessons for
MLM Leaders

TOM "BIG AL" SCHREITER

For information, contact:
Fortune Network Publishing
PO Box 890084
Houston, TX 77289 USA
Telephone: +1 (281) 280-9800
ISBN: 1-892366-24-X
ISBN-13: 978-1-892366-24-5

DEDICATION

This book is dedicated to network marketers everywhere.

I travel the world 240+ days each year. Let me know if you want me to stop in your area and conduct a live Big Al training.

http://www.BigAlSeminars.com

Get 7 mini-reports of amazing, easy sentences that create new, hot prospects.

Sign up today at:

http://www.BigAlReport.com

Other great Big Al Books available at:

http://www.BigAlBooks.com

TABLE OF CONTENTS

PREFACE

In this volume on leadership, Volume Two, we will talk more about some of the activities and lessons we can give to our potential leaders.

Preaching and lecturing do not build leaders. Showing, participating, experiencing and learning stories produce much better results. For anyone who believes that lecturing works, all you have to do is to think back to your teenage years. Lectures from parent and teachers sometimes had little effect.

However, once we experience something, whether externally or in our mind, new beliefs come forward. And hopefully, these beliefs can move our teams much closer to their destinations.

New viewpoints give us new insights. And new insights help us move past our current limitations.

— Tom "Big Al" Schreiter

Why don't distributors make a total commitment to be leaders?

Do you have at least **one** senior sales leader in your organization?

How would you like to have, at the end of next year, **12 senior sales leaders** in your organization?

Okay, here is the plan. It is an **aggressive** plan.

However, if you get this plan working, at the end of the year you will have a powerful organization of developing leaders. (Bet you already figured out what your bonus checks would look like if you had 12 senior sales leaders in your organization!)

Now this is a simple plan ... one new sales leader each and every month. Anybody can do it, even if you mumble, even if you get your sales presentation mixed up and the percentages all wrong.

What you have to do first is find the person who is committed.

In Volume One, I explained a little bit about the three types of commitments.

Let's review:

The first commitment is when a prospect says, **"Well, I will try."** This is the weakest form of commitment. This is the commitment that creates temporary distributors. Your distributor is saying,

"I will **try** this business for a while, and then maybe I will **try** something else if this business doesn't work, I will **try** the lottery, and then maybe I will **try** television for a while. I hope this business doesn't require any work."

It is **not** his fault he thinks this way. Why? Because most people go through their entire life learning to quit. They quit school, they quit their job, they quit their exercise program, they quit their diets.

It is interesting to talk to a distributor and hear a conversation like this:

New Distributor: Hmmm, I'm going to give this a whirl.

Leader: Good. But what happens if you talk to a bunch of people, and they all say, "No?"

New Distributor: Well, I will talk to some more people.

Leader: Good, what happens if you talk to some more people and they say, "No?"

New Distributor: Well, maybe I will work on my presentation and do some training.

Leader: Okay. And what if you talk to some more people, and they all say, "No?"

New Distributor: Well, if nobody wants to join, maybe I will join another company.

Leader: Okay. You join another company, talk to some more people, and they all say, "No." Then what?

New Distributor: Well, I will talk to some more people.

Leader: What if they all say, "No?"

New Distributor: Maybe I will move in with my parents and watch television.

People are professional quitters.

We might as well get used to it.

You can't build a large organization with only distributors. It's impossible to manage and motivate hundreds or thousands of distributors. You need leaders.

The second type of commitment is when the prospect announces, **"I will do the best that I can."** This is much better. Many of our best distributors make this commitment.

Finally there is the third type of commitment, when the prospect promises, **"I will do whatever it takes."** Our potential sales leaders will make this type of commitment.

"I will do whatever it takes" is the commitment you are looking for. These distributors will continue on in the face of adversity and rejection from their family and friends.

They will stay right where they are and focus on whatever it takes to become successful.

That commitment is what makes a potential leader.

The reason our distributors are a little afraid to make a commitment to become a senior sales leader is that in the back of their minds, they wonder:

"What if it **doesn't** come true? What if I stand up and announce to all my relatives that I am going to become a senior sales leader at the end of 30 days? If I don't make my goal, they will make fun of me and mock me for years."

Well, most of our distributors wouldn't be foolhardy enough to make that announcement because they have already anticipated the consequences of failure.

If they failed to become a senior sales leader at the end of 30 days, they would be embarrassed. They would have to eat their words. They would have to listen to their relatives for the rest of their lives reminding them about their failure. Now that is a depressing thought, isn't it?

The guarantee makes the difference.

But what if you could give your distributors an absolutely, positively, 100% guarantee that at the end of 30 days they would be racing towards becoming a senior sales leader?

Do you think this would motivate them? You bet it would!

Do you think they would make that third level of commitment – the **"I will do whatever it takes"** commitment? Yes! In a heartbeat!

So how do you guarantee that a new distributor will become a senior sales leader?

Let's imagine for a moment that you sponsor William. As a brand-new distributor, William suffers from a poor self-image and lacks confidence.

You challenge William by asking him:

"Do you want to work hard and commit to become a sales leader?"

William thinks for a bit. He is new and doesn't want to commit to a project where he will fail, so he gives you a meaningless answer such as:

"Well, maybe I can do it and maybe I can't."

That kind of commitment will **never** work, but you say the **magic phrase** to William:

"William, would you like to be a senior sales leader if you were absolutely, positively 100% guaranteed to succeed?"

And William eagerly replies:

"Well yeah, no problem. Of course I would if my success was guaranteed."

Now that you have William's undivided attention, you tell him about your commitment that will guarantee his success.

The agreement.

You give William the following guarantee:

"Okay William, here is how we are going to do it. You make a part-time commitment of all your **free hours** when you are not working or sleeping. If you spend all that time building your business, I will make a commitment also.

"I will be your upline sponsoring leader. As your upline sponsoring leader, you will have my full-time commitment. Now I am already a senior sales leader, so I know how to get this done.

"But I will also be your **full-time employee**. I will be working not just 40 hours a week, but probably 80 hours a week. Every waking moment I have, I will help you give presentations, and help your downline give presentations. I will help you retail, and help your downline retail. I will help you and your downline give trainings and opportunity meetings.

"And maybe if I find a great prospect sometime during the month, I will help you sponsor that prospect to help build your organization.

"We will work hard and **between your part-time effort and my full-time effort** ... well, I am sure you will be a senior sales leader by the end of the month."

Wow! The odds of William becoming a senior sales leader by the end of the month are pretty good, right? You will have William's part-time concentrated effort plus your full-time effort and experience. It should be easy.

William feels confident because of **your commitment**. He is willing to make the commitment to become a senior sales leader and announce his commitment to the world.

But you really wouldn't want to do this.

Why? Because you can do much, much better than this.

You could say this:

"Okay William, here is how we are going to do it. You make a part-time commitment of all your **free hours** when you are not working or sleeping. If you spend all that time building your business, I will make a commitment also.

"I will be your upline sponsoring leader. As your upline sponsoring leader, you will have my full-time commitment. Now I am already a senior sales leader, so I know how to get this done.

"But I will also be your **full-time employee**. I will be working not just 40 hours a week, but probably 80 hours a week. Every waking moment I have, I will help you give presentations, and help your downline give presentations. I will help you retail, and help your downline retail. I will help you and your downline give trainings and opportunity meetings.

"And maybe if I find a great prospect sometime during the month, I will help you sponsor that prospect to help build your organization.

"We will work hard and **between your part-time effort and my full-time effort** … well, I am sure you will be a senior sales leader by the end of the month.

"But, I also talked to my sponsor, Mary, and I said to her:

'Mary, you know William? Well he is going to be a great distributor. In fact, he is going to be a senior sales leader and he is going to make you a lot of money. William has committed all of his free time for an entire month to concentrate on becoming a senior sales leader. Now, I have already committed to give him a whole month of my full-time effort. So Mary, as my upline sponsor, what can you contribute to help William succeed?'

"Mary said:

'You are right. I am already successful. I am a super gold senior sales leader. You know, I have it all. Quite honestly, I vacation two weeks out of each month. So the maximum amount of time I could set aside to help William would be **two weeks**. I am sure I could do a meeting or two, maybe help with some three-way phone calls, and help William find a few extra prospects.'

"So William, with your part-time commitment, my full-time commitment, plus Mary's two-week commitment, I am sure we will have you to the rank of senior sales leader before the end of the month."

This sounds impressive, but would we stop there?

Now between William's efforts, your efforts, and Mary's efforts, you have a pretty powerful team.

But would you stop there?

Of course not. We would continue to get more commitments from our upline. We want to **overwhelm** William with the commitments of his upline. We want him to have the **immediate confidence** that he will become a senior sales leader by the end of the month.

So maybe we would say this:

"Okay William, here is how we are going to do it. You make a part-time commitment of all your **free hours** when you are not working or sleeping. If you spend all that time building your business, I will make a commitment also.

"I will be your upline sponsoring leader. As your upline sponsoring leader, you will have my full-time commitment. Now I am already a senior sales leader, so I know how to get this done.

"But I will also be your **full-time employee**. I will be working not just 40 hours a week, but probably 80 hours a week. Every waking moment I have, I will help you give presentations, and help your downline give presentations. I will help you retail, and help your downline retail. I will help you and your downline give trainings and opportunity meetings.

"And maybe if I find a great prospect sometime during the month, I will help you sponsor that prospect to help build your organization.

"We will work hard and **between your part-time effort and my full-time effort** ... well, I am sure you will be a senior sales leader by the end of the month.

"But, I also talked to my sponsor, Mary, and I said to her:

'Mary, you know William? He is going to be a great distributor. In fact, he is going to be a senior sales leader and he is going to make you a lot of money. William has committed all of his free time for an entire month to concentrate on becoming a senior sales leader. Now, I have already committed to give him a whole month of my full-time effort. So Mary, as my upline sponsor, what can you contribute to help William succeed?'

"Mary said:

'You are right. I am already successful. I am a super gold senior sales leader. You know, I have it all. Quite honestly, I vacation two weeks out of each month. So the maximum amount of time I could set aside to help William would be **two weeks**. I am sure I could do a meeting or two, maybe help with some three-way phone calls, and help William find a few extra prospects.'

"**And** ... I also talked to Mary's sponsor, Amelia. I told Amelia that you were going to be a senior sales leader and make her a lot of money. I told her how you committed all of your free time for an entire month to concentrate on becoming a senior sales leader. I told her how I committed a whole month of my full-time effort. And I told Amelia that Mary was contributing two weeks of her time to help also.

"I then asked Amelia, 'So what can you do to help? We are putting together a major team effort here to help William become a senior sales leader right away.'

"Amelia said, 'Well, I am a super gold eagle platinum senior sales leader. I worked my way to the top and I vacation three weeks out of the month. So the maximum amount of time I can set aside to help William is one week. I have a great reputation as a powerful leader here in the community, so I am sure that my one week of effort will greatly contribute to this campaign.'

"I accepted Amelia's offer for help ... **but I didn't stop there**. I wanted even more help from our upline. I wanted to guarantee that you would make senior sales leader by the 15th of the month.

"So I talked with Amelia's sponsor, Mark.

"He said, 'Hey, I am a super gold eagle platinum senior sales leader with extra feathers. I vacation four weeks out of the month, I am super successful, and quite honestly, I don't even like seeing you guys around. So - I will give you $500 for a co-op advertising campaign if you get out of here. All right?'

"I took Mark's $500 commitment to help."

So here is the deal.

"William, we have your commitment of all of your part-time hours.

"I will be your full-time employee to help you succeed during this one-month campaign.

"But we also have Mary's two-week commitment. She's a real professional and we're lucky to have her help.

"Plus Mary's upline sponsor, Amelia, is going to give us a big boost with her credibility and her one-week effort.

"And we also have $500 to spend for some advertising that was given to us by Mark.

"William, with all of this help, I am **sure** we will have you to the rank of senior sales leader before the month is half over. We can then take the rest of the month off to celebrate."

Your new distributor will make big commitments if he is guaranteed success.

What did we do? We gathered enough commitments for help so that William knew he would be successful. He didn't have to worry about failure, his self-image, or what his relatives would say. He **knew** he would be successful.

It's easy to make commitments when they are guaranteed.

This is just one example of how powerful commitments can be. We simply organized a S.W.A.T. team of heavy-hitters and leaders into an area to help William.

Could you possibly do this with somebody in your group?

If you do, make sure you are successful.

Why? If you are successful with your first distributor, you will build an incredible aura of power that will **attract** more distributors to make that same commitment.

Let's look at this power.

- Does anyone in your downline have trouble sponsoring?
- Are they afraid that they might be rejected?

- Do they have trouble visualizing themselves as a successful senior sales leader?
- Would their attitude and belief change if they saw how you and your upline team helped William become a senior sales leader?

Yes!

Now they could see how to become successful with your help. They would believe that they could become successful because they wouldn't have to do it all themselves.

Now you don't have to **find** committed distributors. You will be **creating** committed distributors who will come to you.

Someone in your distributor organization will be watching your progress with William and say:

"William just became a senior sales leader in less than 30 days. I would like to be next. I want you to do for me what you did for William."

So the next month you and your S.W.A.T. team help this distributor become a senior sales leader.

The next month, another distributor says:

"Hey, I want to be next. I am willing to make a commitment of all of my free time if you and your team will help me become a senior sales leader."

The next month two or three distributors say:

"Hey, I would like to be next. I am willing to make that commitment."

If you consistently help these committed distributors become senior sales leaders, other distributors are going to see a consistent track record, aren't they? They are going to say:

"I want to be next, I want to be next!"

What happens after six or seven months?

Well, you have a long queue of people saying that they want to be next in line because everything you touch turns to gold. And some of these people are still prospects. They want to join your business because you will work with them – and get results.

They are thinking:

"I want to be the next person you help because you are going to help make me successful. Guaranteed. I don't have to worry about making the commitment. I don't have to worry about being embarrassed, because it is guaranteed I am going to be successful."

Want to make a little extra money on the side?

Here is how:

Let's say that you have ten people waiting for their turn to become a senior sales leader. But, you can only work with one person a month.

You simply go to the seventh or eighth person in line and say:

"For $500 I will move you a little further up the line so I can work with you sooner."

Just kidding.

Of course you **wouldn't** do this.

I just wanted to point out that it is a lot more fun when you have people waiting, eager, and committed to work with you. This sure beats chasing after semi-committed distributors and begging them to go to work.

So there you have it. A guaranteed plan to help William and lots of other distributors in your downline become senior sales leaders.

And do you remember the beginning of this chapter? Didn't you want 12 new senior sales leaders by the end of next year? Here is your plan.

All you have to do is start working with William.

"The one and only right way ..."

I like things to be black and white, right or wrong with no ambiguity. Don't you?

So, wouldn't it be nice if there was **only one right way** to do network marketing?

This would make life simple, but I certainly haven't found the one right way. And, I am not sure why there should be only one right way to do network marketing.

I see many ways of doing our business that work. Every day, people succeed in our business, each doing the business differently.

For example, I hate using the telephone. I am extremely uncomfortable whenever I am in a phone conversation longer than 30 seconds. (If you have ever called me, you already know that I try to make my phone conversations as short as possible.)

So what would happen if my sponsor told me:

"The only way to be successful in network marketing is to mail out an information package and follow up each lead using the telephone."

Or,

"The only way to be successful in network marketing is to send people to your web page and follow up each lead with a three-way telephone call."

Maybe I could force myself to suffer for a month or two, but after a period of continued suffering, I'd look for another way to do the business that was more comfortable for me ... or I would quit.

Imagine if my sponsor told me that using the telephone was the only correct way to do network marketing, and that if I didn't follow my sponsor's system ... I should leave the business.

Well, I would have to leave the business. And my sponsor would lose all the potential business that I could have created.

Is the telephone bad?

No. The telephone is great, but it is **only one way** of building our network marketing businesses. I have sponsored leaders who have built their entire business over the telephone. The process works. I just choose to do network marketing in a more enjoyable way for me.

My favorite method is to sponsor someone across the kitchen table. Maybe it is my preoccupation with food, but that method works great for me.

But what about leaders who build their business by telephone?

If I **forced** them to build their network marketing business across the kitchen table, they would quit. They would hate my system of building a business.

So, I do the smart thing. I allow leaders to build their business in the way that is **most comfortable** for them – using the telephone.

Here are just a few of the ways leaders build their businesses:

1. Opportunity meetings

2. Product parties

3. Person-to-person cold calls

4. Direct mail

5. Newspaper advertising

6. Autoresponders

7. Internet lead capture pages

8. Buying leads

9. Referrals

10. Coupons

11. Postcards

There are many more ways, but you get the point. People are different. Their skills are different. And they can successfully build their businesses in different ways.

I respect all these methods. I don't use them all myself, but I respect them. And, as a leader, I try to learn as much as I can about each method so that I can help new distributors who choose one of these alternate ways of building their businesses.

The biggest service we can render to our new distributors is to help them find **which** method works for them. Then, let's help them **use that method** to build their business successfully.

Network marketing should be fun. We should enjoy our business. So why would you want to ruin your fun by using a business-building method you hate?

Ego and hero worship.

Here is how some leaders make their organizations very uncomfortable. If a specific method works for them, then these leaders believe that method should be imposed on everyone in their organization.

For example, imagine that you are a leader and have built your group by running radio ads for opportunity meetings.

Great! It works for you.

However, being human, you decide that you have found the **one and only secret to success**.

In fact, you insist that everyone in your group must use the exact same method. You want your organization to worship you as the founder of the ultimate network marketing success truth.

Then what happens?

- Soon the radio stations are full of similar ads from your organization.
- Listeners turn off their attention as soon as they hear the overexposed ad.
- Some of your distributors run their own versions of your ad, and those versions don't work very well.
- Prospects with hearing disabilities will never hear of your opportunity.
- Some communities don't get good radio reception.
- Some prospects only watch television.

You get the point. This one ultimate truth isn't so ultimate after all. It won't work for everyone in your network marketing organization.

How systems are created.

Most recruiting systems are based upon a true incident. Unfortunately, it is human nature to take single incidents and believe that they are the ultimate truths.

For example, let's say that I am driving down the expressway one day listening to a "Big Al" training audio. The "Big Al" audio is so captivating, I forget about the traffic and I hit the car in front of me.

We both pull over to the side of the road. The other driver gets out of his car, looks at the damage to the rear of his car, and then he starts walking toward me. He bangs on my window. I open my window and say:

"Hey, check out this cool book, *How to Get Rich without Winning the Lottery.*"

He reads the book in his car while waiting for the police to come and fill out the accident report. After reading the book he tells me:

"Wow! This network marketing business sounds great! How can I join?"

This man eventually becomes the best leader in my group.

And now I have a system!

All of my distributors should get on the expressway and rear-end other cars. That is how I got my best leader. My distributors need to duplicate my successful system. Sounds silly, doesn't it?

But that is how most "systems" are started. Someone had a successful experience and now believes that everyone can have the same successful experience.

The duplication myth.

I am not sure who started the rumor that your downline must be able to duplicate everything you do.

If you are limited to prospecting and sponsoring activities that are easily duplicated by your downline, you might be missing some giant possibilities.

There is no need to **insist** on blind duplication of your activities other than to get your ego massaged.

It is okay to use different activities and methods to achieve the results you want.

- Just because you don't conduct opportunity meetings, doesn't mean that your organization should be banned from using this proven activity in their business.
- Just because you don't contact referrals, doesn't mean that your organization should be banned from using this proven activity in their business.
- Just because you don't contact and sponsor your relatives, doesn't mean that your organization should be banned from using this proven activity in their business.

Use your natural advantages.

Some people have natural strengths and talents and should take advantage of them to build their network marketing organizations.

One of my friends has 10,000 people on his mailing list of customers who know, like and trust him. What am I going to say to him?

"Don't mail or contact your customers. Sure, lots of them would love to join and be in your business, but that method doesn't duplicate easily! No one else has 10,000 customers. Don't do it. You are setting a bad example."

I don't think I could tell my friend that. That would be silly. Instead, I would encourage my friend to contact his natural market even though few people could duplicate his method.

What about someone who is a great speaker who motivates crowds to his cause? If your system insists that all activities be conducted one-on-one, across the kitchen table, aren't you doing your speaker-distributor a disservice by not allowing him to use his natural talents to build his business?

The key difference.

What we really need to duplicate are ... results!

What are the results we are looking for in network marketing?

We want to:

"Sponsor distributors and make them successful."

If we focus on results, we can allow people the freedom to achieve those results in many different ways.

- Some will achieve results by contacting prospects by email.
- Some will achieve results by giving product parties.
- Some will achieve results by wearing three-piece suits and conducting opportunity meetings.
- And some people will achieve these results even in Bermuda shorts at the beach.

The bottom line is:

Don't worry about duplicating activities.

Focus on duplicating results.

Why techniques and rigid systems don't matter.

In the end, it is not so much **what** you do - it is **who** you are.

Have you ever seen a new distributor excited about your opportunity? Your new distributor will make many mistakes and **still** sponsor lots of people.

Why?

Enthusiasm. Trust. Personal belief.

These things radiate through your new distributor's presentation so loudly that the prospect doesn't care about the business details. Prospects join because of who you are.

They don't join because your marketing plan pays 4% on level three in the alternate months, or because your product has 21 different certifications from 21 different countries.

Prospects buy **you** ... not your company.

How do you learn the sponsoring technique that is right for you?

I learned from personal trial and error. It's a great way to learn.

Unfortunately, trial and error has two drawbacks:

1. It takes a long time to try and test different techniques. It could take years of trial and error and you may end up with scars all over your heart and mind. If you have a lot of time and can wait a few years to get your business started, then you are one of the fortunate few. Most of us want results a bit faster.

2. It is expensive to fund all of your trial and error campaigns. Very expensive. If you have money to burn, or just enjoy being poor and abused by credit card collectors, then it is not so bad. However, most of us hate to waste money.

Those are the only two things I have against the trial and error method of finding a good sponsoring technique that works for you!

There is a better way.

Read some books. Attend seminars. Consult with your sponsor. And listen to some audio recordings of people who have gone before you (check to see if they have scar tissue.)

Why beat yourself up and spend lots of money when you can read or listen to the results of leaders who have gone before you?

Capitalize on the experience of others! Learn how they approach the different methods of prospecting and sponsoring.

You and your potential leaders are smart enough to pick out the techniques they enjoy.

As my good friend, Tom Paredes, says,

"Even if you go to work at McDonald's flipping hamburgers, they still make you go through their training program."

Our business is more complicated than flipping hamburgers. Don't you think it makes sense to learn or be aware of the many different ways to conduct our business?

What is the ultimate secret to network marketing success?

It is to build **leaders** and help them become successful.

Distributors come and go. It is the leaders who count! You want to develop a few good loyal leaders and then, if you choose, you can retire.

If I had my entire career to do all over again, I would concentrate on building and developing one leader each year.

We talk about the cumulative effect of our efforts in network marketing. Well, **only leaders accumulate**. That is why you should focus your effort into developing leaders.

I have a friend who started with me in network marketing many years ago. We lost touch for over 20 years. During the 20 years we were separated, we both worked hard in network marketing.

When we finally met again, I had a self-sustaining, large and profitable organization. He was starting all over again.

The difference?

I had developed some leaders during my 20 years of hard work. He had sponsored distributors during his 20 years of hard work. We both worked hard.

Twenty years later he had no organization. He was starting over.

While there is really **no one right way** to build your network marketing organization, you can at least focus on this:

1. Help your new distributors find which prospecting and sponsoring method works for them.

2. Then, help them become leaders doing what they do best.

Let's not get caught up in **which** activity our organization uses to build their business, but instead, concentrate on their results.

Who are the best <u>potential</u> leaders to sponsor into your business?

When prospecting, you will want to look for that important ingredient – motivation.

Many people have **skills,** but no **motivation.**

For instance, you may know a bank vice-president with many contacts, a wonderful personality, and terrific people skills. Yet, even though the bank vice-president has many skills, you don't have a potential leader if he isn't **motivated** for a change in his life.

Who would be the best prospects?

Prospects with an **intense desire for change.** Some prospects want to leave a boring factory job, a high-pressure sales job, or a dead-end career. When you offer an opportunity for change, they will have total motivation, 100% of the time.

You won't have to send them a motivational tip of the day. You won't have to console them because a prospect didn't join. These select potential leaders have a built-in, sustainable motivation. In other words, they won't need a constant reminder of why they are working the business.

Plus, highly motivated potential leaders don't need super skills. Because of their built-in motivation, they will always find a way to learn the skills to get the job done.

The most motivated prospect with mediocre skills will always out-perform the unmotivated prospect with super skills.

Remember, look for **motivation** when prospecting for your potential leaders, not **skills**.

1. Skills can be taught.

2. Motivation is much hard to transfer to a distributor.

Your distributors invest time and money for training ... and then do nothing.

One of the leadership principles we must follow is:

"It is never a matter of skill, it is always a matter of desire."

In other words, no matter how much skill a distributor possesses, if the distributor is not motivated, **nothing happens.**

Have you ever seen this occur in your business?

Let's say you have a brand-new distributor. Your new distributor hasn't had the time to attend training and learn about all the ingredients of each product. Your new distributor didn't read a single page of the distributor manual. (Sound familiar?)

However, your new distributor is excited!

Why?

This is the chance of a lifetime to build a business, quit the old job, travel, spend time with the family and to really dream and enjoy life. Your excited distributor talks to everyone.

The result?

Lots of new distributors sponsored the very first month. Your brand-new distributor has an excited, growing group. And, your brand-new distributor still **doesn't know anything** about his business.

What about the experienced professional?

Let's say you have an experienced, knowledgeable, five-years-of-experience distributor in your group. He has accumulated all the knowledge in the world, all the training in the world, and all of the skills necessary to build a powerful organization.

However, during the very same month that your new distributor sponsored lots of new distributors, your experienced distributor **did not** sponsor a single person!

Even though your experienced distributor possessed all of the knowledge, all of the training, and all of the skills, **nothing happened.**

What was the difference?

Desire.

Desire is what lights up that inner motivation.

When a person has motivation, things happen. You see, it is not important if the distributor has the right closing statement or brochure. What is important is that the distributor has the desire to sponsor new people.

If your desire is great enough, you will figure out a way to get the job done.

A good example is swimming. If you didn't know how to swim, what would you do if you accidentally fell into the deep end of the local swimming pool?

Would you paddle furiously and struggle to the pool's edge?

You bet!

Even though you didn't have the skill to swim, your desire to continue living motivated you to dog-paddle, kick, and struggle your way to safety. You had desire!

Quick! Give me a manual on how to swim.

What you **didn't** say when you fell in the pool was this:

- "I never took swimming lessons before. When is the next opportunity to register for lessons?"

- "Could you please hand me a book on swimming? I would like to study it now."
- "I will probably drown because my sponsor lives too far away."
- "The company back-ordered the swimming skill video? Well, I might as well quit now and drown."
- "My upline never held swimming skill lessons at convenient times. It is his fault that I am going to drown."
- "I didn't have to learn to swim with my last company. Why should they require me to learn now?"
- "The ad said, 'All you have to do is join, we will do all the rest. We will sponsor, train, and build your organization for you. You won't even have to learn to swim.'"

No, you did not say any of the above excuses. When you have desire, none of the previous excuses mean a thing. You just figured out a way to achieve your goal, even if you didn't have the knowledge, training or skills to get the job done. With desire, everything is possible.

The Dave Test.

My good friend, Dave, networks and sells a service.

Dave says his company provides the new distributor with an excellent training kit, packed with great knowledge and information. Many new distributors take the kit home, study it, digest it, outline key points, ponder the training techniques, and well, **they never go out and talk to their first prospect**.

So Dave tried this experiment.

Instead of giving some new distributors the kit right away, Dave only gave these distributors some service sign-up forms for customers. The new distributors went to their prospects, asked them to try their service, filled out the forms, and then ...

They came back to Dave to ask him for more sign-up forms!

These new distributors immediately got into action. Instead of studying and pondering, they went out and got the job done. Now maybe these new distributors didn't have all the answers, and maybe they didn't have all the skills, but they still got the job done.

They wanted to build their networking business.

What's the point?

I am not saying that you should hide the distributor kits. Dave just did that for this experiment to prove a point. The real lesson here is:

Don't blame inactivity on lack of skill training. Blame inactivity on lack of desire.

What does this mean to leaders? What can we learn from Dave's experiment with desire?

Maybe we can change **what** we do as leaders.

Maybe it is more important to **create desire** and to give new distributors a **vision**.

Maybe it's less important to give new distributors all of the step-by-step skills to get the job done.

Now, think back to your last training program.

How did you use your time?

Did you spend most of your time helping your distributors create desire? Or, did you spend most of your time teaching information?

If your training session was like most training sessions, the time was spent on:

- Understanding the percentage payout on Level Four when the bonus qualification is equal to Zone Three.
- The types of antioxidants and the most recent testing for effectiveness when the body's pH is alkaline.
- Learning how to coordinate the flip chart with your memorized presentation.
- Mastering the four types of hard closes and the three types of trial closes.
- Looking at slides and statistics showing that the market for network marketing services will grow 80% in the next four years.
- The seven different ways to fill out the form while your prospect is off-guard.

- How to manipulate the compensation plan to get the last cent in commissions.

Now, all of this is okay. It's great to know these things. And, your distributor should learn skills.

However, if your distributor is not motivated, he will keep all this knowledge and skill ... **top secret!**

That's right. If your distributor's motivation and desire is not **greater** than his fear of rejection, then nothing will happen.

And that's why much of our training time is wasted. We train our distributors for situations that will never happen.

Our distributors will never come in contact with a prospect ... unless they have desire.

What is the solution?

I'm not saying you should withhold information and skills from your distributor.

What I am saying is: "Make sure you help your new distributor **find a motivating reason** to build his business."

You'll want to find a motivating reason that is so big that it makes the fear of rejection appear small and insignificant. This is how you get new distributors to jump into action.

How can we get our distributors to focus on a compelling reason to get excited?

Ask questions.

You will get your distributors to think hard when you ask razor-sharp, insightful questions.

What can you ask?

Almost any question will be better than no question. And note, the question is not nearly as important as the answer. Make sure you give your new distributor time to ponder and weigh his answers. **The magic is in the answer**, not in the question.

Here are some ideas for questions to ask:

- When your bonus check starts growing, what are you going to do with the money?
- Who would be especially proud of you when you build a large and successful business?
- What are your favorite hobbies?
- How much time do you spend at work, and how much time do you spend with your family?
- If you didn't have to go to work, how would you spend that time?
- Who could you help most by being successful in this business?
- How do you see yourself five years from now?
- What is the most important reason you want to work this business?

These are just sample questions. Put together some questions of your own that you are comfortable with.

Once you have located that burning desire, the reason why your distributor wants to do the business, then your job gets a lot easier.

For example, let's imagine that your new distributor wants to build a large and successful networking business.

Why?

To get even with his overbearing, rude, bragging brother-in-law. Your new distributor wants to earn enough money to buy an overpowered sports car with fat tires. Then, your new distributor plans to spin the wheels up and down his brother-in-law's driveway and leave black rubber marks everywhere.

Now, you may not agree with your new distributor's motivation, but that is not your job. Your job is to support and help your new distributor and allow him the freedom to choose why he wants to do the business.

Here is how your job gets easier. Because you know your new distributor's burning desire, obstacles and objections are easy to overcome. For instance:

Objection: I don't think I want to go to the meeting. It is raining outside.

You: But you do want to leave those black rubber marks up and down your brother-in-law's driveway, don't you?

Your new distributor instantly un-focuses on the objection and instantly re-focuses on his reason to build the business.

Once you know the reason your new distributor wants to succeed, you can use the same answer on almost any objection.

Objection: The company might raise prices again.

You: But you do want to leave those black rubber marks up and down your brother-in-law's driveway, don't you?

Objection: My best distributor quit. Maybe I should stay home.

You: But you do want to leave those black rubber marks up and down your brother-in-law's driveway, don't you?

Objection: It's not fair that Mary got to speak longer at the last meeting.

You: But you do want to leave those black rubber marks up and down your brother-in-law's driveway, don't you?

Objection: This seems hard to do.

You: But you do want to leave those black rubber marks up and down your brother-in-law's driveway, don't you?

If your new distributor's desire is big enough, no objection, no obstacle, no lack of training or skills will keep him away from success.

Remember, your new distributor doesn't know how important desire is. You do.

Can you recruit 100 people in one week?

During one of my marketing workshops, I asked how many people in the room could recruit 100 people in the coming week. The room was full, yet **not a single hand was raised.**

I then pulled out my checkbook and pen, and asked:

"How many people in this room could recruit 100 people in the coming week if you had a check made out in your name for $50,000 just waiting for you?"

This time about half of the people in the room quickly raised their hands.

What changed?

It wasn't money motivation or any incentive that changed their minds, because they hadn't received the money or incentive yet.

The only thing that changed was this:

They changed their minds from thinking **"I can't"** to thinking **"I can."**

And changing one's mind doesn't cost a cent.

What if they say No?

Even **uneducated action** is better than attending training for several years with no action.

Do you have distributors who are still waiting to get started in the business? Do they constantly have one more excuse why they can't start right now?

I learned this from one of the smartest networkers I know, Richard Brooke. He wrote the book, *The Four Year Career: How to Make Your Dreams of Fun and Financial Freedom Come True ... Or Not.*

If you ask Richard:

"Who do I talk to, what do I say, and what if they say, 'No'?"

Richard has a simple answer. And I love his answer. His answer finishes the conversation and the new distributor sees the business the way we see the business.

Here is what Richard says:

"Look, what if instead of you becoming a distributor, we just hire you. Here is your job: go talk to two people a day, five days a week, for four years. It does not matter if they join the business. It does not matter what they ask, or what their objections are – just respond to the best of your ability and go with the flow, no matter what.

"If you fail to talk to two people a day, you will be fired, and can't come to work for us again. Got that?

"We won't pay you a nickel for the first four years. But if you haven't missed a day at the end of four years, we will pay you $100,000 a year for the rest of your life, no matter what you do."

Could you perform on that contract?

Anyone could.

Suddenly, all of your distributor's questions are answered. He sees what you see.

Who is your distributor going to talk to? Anybody.

What will your distributor say? Whatever comes to mind.

What if the prospect says, "No?" Your distributor has four years' worth of prospects to choose from.

You see ...

"It is never a matter of skill, it is always a matter of desire."

Instant leaders, instant success.

Instant success in network marketing is rare. And when instant success occurs, there is usually a reason. Remember, things are not always as they appear.

Many times you will hear a speaker at an event or opportunity meeting say:

"I just joined, talked to a few people, and by golly, in just one month I reached the top level of achievement, and they needed a truck to deliver my giant-sized bonus check. Anybody can do this business."

Well, what the speaker said may be true. She did reach the top and it was fast. Unfortunately, because of **time constraints** on the meeting, the speaker didn't get to tell the whole story.

You see, the reason the speaker sponsored such a big downline in her organization in only 30 days was:

1. She had 20 years of previous experience in network marketing. She had lots of contacts, relationships and friends who knew her, trusted her, and respected her. Since they also were experienced network marketers, they were able to sponsor many distributors quickly also. The speaker

had **20 years of preparation** for this so-called "one-month flash of success."

2. Or maybe the speaker went door-to-door in her city and everyone she talked to joined her program. Too bad there wasn't enough time during the meeting to mention that her mother was mayor of the town, owned all the houses, and that the tenants felt obligated to do whatever her daughter suggested.

3. The speaker worked as an assistant teacher for 40 years in the community. She also taught junior high sports. Everyone in town knows her, trusts her, and respects her. In fact, she taught most of the town's residents. How could you say "No" to the person who used to make you clean the erasers?

Instant success?

I don't think so.

You have to earn your success in network marketing. That is why some people grow faster than others.

So, if you don't have any friends, people hate you, and no one respects you, well, you will just have to start building some new relationships to get your business started. Once you have built the relationships, your business will grow. **Networking is done with people who trust you.** If you don't have anyone to network with, go out and build some trust.

So is that why some people become an instant success?

Yes.

They have **already** been networking for years and years.

Consider this. When I started my network marketing career, I lived in a new city where I knew few people. I was an introvert. No social life, no outside activities. I had no "warm market" prospects.

No wonder it was so hard for me to get started. I was socially-challenged, shy, and knew no one.

But I had a friend named John. He started at the same time that I did. He built an instant group. Why?

He had lived in our city all his life. He was outgoing and had many outside activities with other groups of people. He had a **25-year head start** on me in his network marketing career. No wonder his group grew so quickly, while I wondered what was happening.

I had to carefully and methodically build new contacts and new relationships. Plus I had to get a personality too.

Is there a prospecting lesson here?

Oh yes. A big lesson.

If you sponsor **experienced** networkers into your business, your business will grow quickly.

Now, here is what I mean by **experienced** networkers. These people have been networking all their lives. You will find these people in professions such as:

1. Wedding planners

2. Insurance agents

3. Ministers

4. Politicians

5. Salesmen

6. Teachers

7. Real estate agents, etc.

You want to sponsor people who have **already** done the hardest part of network marketing, building a list of prospects that know, like and trust them. This takes time. And this also takes some social skills. So to build faster, just think:

"Who do I know that is an **experienced** networker?"

"There are two types of people in the world."

Only two?

I like to look at people as belonging to one of these two groups.

1. Those people who look for reasons why things can work.

2. Those people who look for reasons why things can't work.

You see these people every day of your life. They create their own happiness and success, or ... they create their own frustration, sadness and spend their time acting like a victim of all the bad things life brings them.

How things work in the real world of network marketing.

Mary drives to work and encounters a huge traffic jam. She thinks,

"It is a beautiful day. The sun is shining. Let me listen to the new release of my favorite musical artist."

Ben drives to work also. He happens to be in the same traffic jam as Mary. He thinks,

"Look at this traffic jam. Why doesn't the government build wider roads? What idiot planned this road repair during rush hour? I am wasting my time sitting here in this traffic. I will be late for work. Let me complain and blow my horn for the next 15 minutes."

Ben pushes the horn down and it blares a continuous and irritating noise. Ben is furious. In front of Ben, the driver gets tired of listening to Ben's horn. He gets out of his car, grabs his tire wrench, walks back to Ben's car ... and **smashes** Ben's windshield!

Now Ben is really upset.

He thinks,

"Look at that! Not only am I stuck in traffic, my windshield has been vandalized! There are never any police officers around when you need them. I pay taxes and never get the police protection I need. I am such a **victim**. The world keeps **sabotaging** me. How can I get to work with a broken windshield? It's not **my** fault. The government should protect me from these vandals!"

Needless to say, Ben leads a life of **personal sabotage** and suffering. He literally **creates** the results in his life, but never realizes that his circumstances are **self-induced**. Instead, Ben blames the economy, the government, his family, his friends, his job, the weather, the rules, his upline, his downline, the company, and his disloyal dog!

All of Ben's energies are spent **trying to get the world to change.**

Ben is a professional victim, and the world should feel sorry for him and fix everything for him.

Ben arrived at work cursing at the terrible circumstances he had endured. Ben's co-workers quietly turned their backs and ignored Ben. They didn't want to join, or be a part of, Ben's world.

But wait!

What about Mary?

Mary is in the same traffic jam. She has the same opportunity as Ben.

So what did Mary do with her opportunity?

She **chose** to enjoy life. To listen to her favorite music. To enjoy the beautiful day. She arrived at work with a smile.

Mary's co-workers crowded around Mary. They enjoyed Mary's companionship. They **wanted** to be part of Mary's world.

Mary had the **same** network marketing opportunity as Ben. She **created** her results. People were **attracted** to Mary. They **wanted** to be associated with Mary.

Here is what I find so interesting.

Mary didn't change her circumstances. She didn't get the government to build wider roads. She didn't blame her upline, downline, company or dog. All Mary did was choose her personal actions. And choosing one's personal actions is entirely within our control.

Ben attempted to make the world change. He felt he couldn't be happy or successful unless everything changed. He blamed the government, his upline, his downline, the company, and his dog. Ben felt **powerless.** Ben felt he was a victim. Ben felt weak and that he didn't have the power to choose his personal actions. And Ben felt that when people avoided him, it had nothing to do with him. It was always everyone else's fault.

So what could the world do for Ben?

Nothing.

Even if someone changed the weather, switched dogs, or widened the roads, Ben would still feel like a powerless victim, and would continue to look for more signs that the world was "out to get him."

Ben would interpret the next stop sign as a vicious plot to impede his success. There is nothing you or the world can do to help Ben. He will continue to snatch defeat from the jaws of victory.

If you bought Ben a first-class ticket to heaven, he would only complain about altitude sickness.

Ben never understands that the world he lives in … **is created by him.**

When you run across the Bens of the world, what should you do? You know that they will only look for the "reasons things can't work."

For the Bens in your life, instead of attempting to change everything in the world, try concentrating on changing their outlook toward the world.

Now, this is a full-time job even for the best-trained psychologists, so don't get totally tied up in the missionary work of changing the Bens of the world. This would be a low-paying, frustrating profession.

But maybe you could loan the Bens of the world a few audios and see if they will take the first step away from being professional victims. You can't afford to waste your life getting sucked into the black hole of their lives.

When you run across the Marys of the world, what should you do?

Celebrate!

The Marys of the world have already learned that if they look for reasons "why things will work," then prospects will naturally be **attracted** to them. They will have crowds of prospects waiting to be associated with them. They won't have to run ads, cold-call prospects on the phone, or beg strangers to join them. They create an atmosphere that attracts like-minded people.

And your decision will be?

Since today is available to everyone, which choice are you going to make?

Will you make the same choice as Ben?

Then you will experience loneliness, frustration, and depression. Running one more ad for prospects **won't** make a difference. No one wants to follow a leader on a suicide mission.

Or, will you make the same choice as Mary?

Then you will experience joy, wealth, satisfying relationships, and a more successful business.

"We can make the world a better place to live, but we can't make it a happier place to live."

You can work 24 hours a day to make things better for your distributors. You can find new solutions to their problems.

But, you can't make people happy.

No matter what you do, people can choose to be happy about it, or sad about it. It is their personal choice.

If your company changes the product label color from blue to green, everyone can choose how they react to this event.

We want potential leaders to know that no matter how hard they try, some people won't join, some people won't come, and some of their distributors will think that they don't do enough.

If someone is unhappy, that is his or her choice. We can choose to be happy about most events if we desire to. Changing the events and changing the problems won't guarantee that people will be happy.

Happiness in others is not within your control. As you can see in the following example, only others can determine how happy or sad they will be.

* * *

During our annual Thanksgiving networking cruise, I observed a good example of why some people are **doomed for failure** in network marketing.

I was standing in the buffet line. Two men were talking. This was their conversation:

Man #1: I can't believe how quiet and peaceful it is today. It is beautiful, just beautiful.

Man #2: Nothing is happening on this cruise. It is boring. What a waste of time.

Man #1: Hey look! There are three different types of shrimp for appetizers.

Man #2: The food on this cruise isn't nearly as good as my last vacation. I don't know how they could serve this stuff.

Man #1: I think I will take three desserts with me on this trip in the buffet line.

Man #2: My room steward is rude and I don't like the way he cleans up my room. And my shower water is too hot.

Man #1: I am looking forward to the Las Vegas show tonight. Want to come with me? We can get front row seats if we go 15 minutes early.

Man #2: No way! The music is too loud and all that singing and dancing ... I could watch that on television if I was interested.

Man #1: Let's get some ice cream. It is all-you-can-eat!

Man #2: That stuff just makes you fat. I've tasted better ice cream at my local delicatessen.

Man #1: I just love cruising. It's a great way to get away and relax.

Man #2: I'm homesick already. It is boring. The bartender doesn't smile at me. The sun is too hot. There are too many activities. Everyone is running around with irritating smiles on their faces. You can't get a decent newspaper and I don't like the free movies they are showing tonight. My travel agent charged me too much.

The captain isn't going where I want to go. The swimming pools make me wet ...

* * *

So what's the bottom line?

There is nothing your business, your upline, your downline, or your dog can do to change what you are experiencing in your life.

The good news is that you can choose to control what you are experiencing in your life.

The bad news is that you might not.

Creating a different viewpoint.

Your distributor whines:

"I can't see how I can make any money. I mean, I drive across town, hope to meet a prospect, buy him coffee, leave him some materials ... and then, **if** he joins, I will only make $10 in overrides a month. That will barely pay for the gas and coffee! This just doesn't get me excited."

And the distributor is right. That's not very exciting. You can't buy much today with only $10.

And it's all our fault.

You see, we gave the distributor the wrong viewpoint in our training. It is **what we say and what we do** that makes the difference when training new distributors.

Just a simple repositioning of our training could have made our distributor excited. All we had to do is to put the $10 monthly bonus into **yearly** terms. It sounds better when we say:

"And every time a prospect joins, you could earn up to $120 in bonuses in just the first year, with the chance of earning much, much more in years to come. That's a pretty good payoff for just a few minutes of your time and a cup of coffee."

See the difference? It is **what we say and what we do.**

Or, how about this example from Wes Linden in England. Wes sells utilities. He made a post on Facebook that said:

"I spent 35 minutes showing a friend of my dad how to save some money on her bills. Yesterday I got paid for that 35-minute conversation for the 194th time."

What a great way to reposition our distributor's thinking in just a few words.

And, that is also a great way to explain residual income versus the linear/job, one-time income.

Teaching distributors how to change their prospects' beliefs.

Once you re-educate your prospects, their lives will never be the same. Why?

People tend to notice things that support their beliefs. When you give people new knowledge, new beliefs, and new points of view, they will constantly see facts that support your business proposition. That means just one simple follow-up call or contact can skyrocket your results.

How does this new point of view work?

For example, you are driving down the highway. Lots and lots of cars pass by. Some Corvettes, some BMWs, some Kias (rather slowly), some Fords, etc. Lots and lots of cars.

Do you notice them? Not really.

Now, imagine you purchase a brand-new Mercedes. You travel the same highway and pass the same cars as the day before. Did you notice all the Mercedes cars? Sure. Because now you drive a Mercedes. You now notice **each** Mercedes you pass. You have a new point of view regarding Mercedes cars.

Another example. Let's say you think that all of the people in the neighboring city are idiots, jerks, morons and wasted humanity. You notice every mistake they make and you say to yourself, "Yep. There they go again. What a bunch of losers." Your consciousness goes out of its way to locate instances that support your belief.

We see example after example of this phenomenon every day.

- If a woman has a bad experience with a man (rare, but still possible), will she tend to think all men are jerks and notice events that prove her point?
- If a man buys a foreign car that turns out to be a lemon, won't he constantly find instances of cheap, low-quality foreign goods?
- If you believe today is going to be a great day, won't you notice the beautiful sunshine and gorgeous scenery?
- If you believe today is going to be a terrible day, won't you notice the traffic jams, the garbage on the streets and the sad faces of people going to work?

The point is this:

People usually experience what they believe.

Their minds seek out instances of proof to support their beliefs.

Is this a recent human phenomenon? No.

Here's a quote from Isaac Asimov's *Book of Facts*:

"Abraham Lincoln was convinced all his life that he, like his mother, Nancy Hanks, was illegitimate, and he observed that 'bastards are generally smarter, shrewder, and more intelligent than others.' Not until after his assassination was it proved that Lincoln had been legitimate."

So even President Abraham Lincoln sought out experiences that justified his beliefs.

Okay, okay. You are thinking, "Yes, that's a nice psychological phenomenon ... yawn. How will that help my business?"

Immensely!

All you have to do is ... give your prospect a new belief and your prospect will find experiences to prove you right. That's right. Your prospect will do all the work for you.

Want to see how this works?

Let's say you have a neighbor that goes to work every day. His belief? You have to go to work every day to earn a living. Your neighbor doesn't believe in network marketing. Network marketing is too unconventional. You can't make money if you don't have a real job.

Our task is to gradually give our neighbor a new belief. We don't want to beg or force our opportunity on our neighbor. We want our neighbor to volunteer to go to an opportunity meeting.

Here is how we do it.

One morning say to your neighbor,

"Morning, Neighbor. Glad to see you are off for another day at work. Hey, did you ever look out your window at work? Did you notice all those people running around on the streets and sidewalks? When you go to lunch over at the mall, did you notice all those shoppers? I wonder what they do for a living since they don't go to a regular job?"

You just planted the seed.

Your neighbor sees a bunch of happy shoppers while he is at lunch. He thinks, "Do they have different hours? Do they own their own business? How is it they have time off for shopping during a weekday?"

When your neighbor looks out the office window, he sees people playing in the park. He thinks, "Not all of those people can be millionaires or retirees. How do they earn a living and still have time to play in the park?"

Everywhere your neighbor looks, he sees people who are not going to work. Lots of independent people. Lots of happy people. Now, these people were there every day, but your neighbor just didn't notice them, until you gave your neighbor a new belief.

Time to collect.

One week later you see your neighbor come home from work. You say,

"Howdy, Neighbor. Long day at the office, eh? Have you ever considered a part-time or full-time business so you would have more time to do what you really want?"

Your question now has validity, it's real. Your prospect saw hundreds of people this past week who aren't tied down to a 9-to-5 job. In fact, everywhere your neighbor looked, he saw people who were enjoying themselves and who weren't locked up in an office building.

What is the attitude and response to your prospecting question from your neighbor? He thinks, "Lots of people have time off during the day and still make a living. Why not check out this part-time business thing?"

See the difference? If you ask the recruiting question of your neighbor **before** he has the new belief, you are shot down in flames. Your job is to simply change the prospect's beliefs. The rest is easy.

Professional marketers know that when they change the prospects' beliefs, the prospects will come to them.

Want some more examples? Here are some prospect beliefs that may hold back your business:

1. You can't lose weight with pills or shakes.

2. Nobody makes money in network marketing.

3. Only the people at the top make the big money.

4. Network marketing is door-to-door sales.

5. You have to be an extrovert to earn big money in network marketing.

6. I don't have time for anything.

7. My friends will think poorly of me if I try this.

8. Jobs have security, network marketing doesn't.

9. My company really appreciates and values my work.

10. Pyramids are illegal.

11. The government will take care of me.

See the picture?

All of these beliefs are holding back your prospects, preventing them from cashing in on the freedom and money that network marketing provides. When we change these beliefs, the prospects will form a line at our front door, asking to join our opportunity.

Beliefs are easier to change than you think. Don't ever believe that you can't change people's beliefs. You can. Of course you can't change all the people's beliefs all the time, and you can't change every belief a person has. You only need to change a few prospects' beliefs and you can literally make a fortune in network marketing.

Using vivid language to change beliefs.

Loyal leaders are home-grown, inside your organization. We want to take ordinary people and teach them the step-by-step, word-for-word things to say and do.

Here is an example to teach potential leaders how to conduct interesting conversations and presentations.

If your potential leader just gives the facts, the listeners will be thinking:

"You are boring. You are not flamboyant. You are not energetic. Did you have a charisma bypass operation? You never move a single step. Are you frozen? Have you ever considered movement or a hand gesture?"

This is not the conversation we want in the heads of listeners. The solution?

Relating to listeners in graphic and picturesque words that they can easily see in their own lives.

If your potential leader can get listeners and prospects to be able to **see what he or she sees** ... well, that is great communication.

Want an example?

Most speakers would say:

"You are what you eat. Good nutrition will make you feel better."

While this is true, the listeners won't internalize this statement. The listeners will simply think that the information is nice, but they won't change their thinking or their lives based upon this boring information.

How could your potential leader present this same information?

Instead of saying:

"You are what you eat. Good nutrition will make you feel better."

Why not say something like this?

***

"Guess what your body is made of? It is not made up of the air you breathe or the friends you associate with. It is made up of what you eat.

"Now, for some of you, this could mean your body is made up of colas and donuts. You know who you are. But you might still be skeptical, so take this test.

"How you **feel** depends on what you eat. I can prove it.

"If you eat a large two-pound steak, how do you feel a few hours later? Lazy. Tired. Lethargic.

"If you eat six donuts, how do you feel 30 minutes later? Wired. Full of nervous energy. And how do you feel one hour later? Lazy. Tired. Lethargic.

"If you eat Chinese food, how do you feel one hour later? Hungry.

"If you drink a six-pack of beer, how do you feel one hour later? Lazy. Tired. Lethargic. Sleepy. Mellow.

"If you drink six cups of coffee, how do you feel one hour later? Edgy. Nervous. Irritable.

"If you eat a half-dozen hot jalapeno peppers, how do you feel one hour later? Warm. Burning sensation. And how do you feel the next day? Warm again as they pass through your system.

"So as you see, how you **feel** depends on what you eat."

***

Now, the listener is **convinced** that what he eats will determine how he feels.

It is not just someone giving a sales pitch. The listener relates to the examples and sees the truth in his life. The difference is huge. Leaders have to be great communicators.

Now when the listener sits down and eats six donuts, and washes them down with a six-pack of beer, he will be thinking of your potential leader and what he said.

And that's exactly what you want.

We can't expect ordinary distributors to magically have leadership skills when they join, so it is up to us to teach them exactly what to say.

We want to teach them how to use "sound bites" and "word pictures" to make their messages ultra-effective.

To illustrate this, let's use a typical sales presentation about joining our opportunity. Instead of us saying:

"Here is your chance to build a business and quit your job,"

We could add some vivid language to make the message more memorable. We could say:

***

"If you are like most of us, waking up to an alarm clock is pure torture. I bet we would all like to sell our alarm clocks to our neighbors. Why?

"Because the alarm clock means we have to leave our families and rush to work, where our dream-sucking vampire boss is going to drain the life out of us. And then we have to fight traffic and commute back home, exhausted.

"So why not start the countdown to firing your boss and getting rid of your old life right now? Nobody wants to extend their alarm clock sentence."

***

Is there a difference in the second explanation? Of course. We need to point out to our potential leader that learning the skill of communicating our message is an important skill to master.

How to help prospects relate to your presentation.

How about some small, bite-sized tips that you can put to use in your presentation right away? As leaders, we all give presentations, so let's make our presentations come alive.

Here are some of my favorite presentation phrases and segments that get prospects to **think.** (And a few for the distributors to think about also.)

Remember that our prospects will only remember a point or two about our presentation, so let's make our points stand out in their minds.

Preparing the prospects.

"There are two types of people in the world. Those who look for reasons why, and those who look for reasons why not."

This puts the prospects in an "open-minded" attitude. They will naturally look for reasons why this opportunity can work for them instead of looking for reasons not to join.

When I use this phrase to start a presentation, I notice that I don't have to use any pressure or closing techniques. Because the prospects are open-minded, no manipulation to open their minds is needed. They can fairly judge for themselves if this opportunity can fill their needs or not.

I don't have time.

"Most people spend about three hours a week complaining about their jobs and stupid bosses. Another hour per week is spent discussing bad decisions from politicians. And there is the time spent discussing in-laws."

Most prospects smile and realize that they could use a few minutes of this non-productive time to build a networking business. I don't ask prospects to give up this chatter time with their friends. I simply ask them to **change** the subject of their chatter for a few minutes.

Everyone has 24 hours in a day. It is how we choose to use those 24 hours that counts. I can't give prospects more time, but I can give them an option of what they can do with some of their time.

Will I fail?

"Let's say that you have a one-year-old child who is just learning to walk. After the child falls, you say, 'Okay. That's it. Don't you ever try again.'

"You wouldn't say that, would you? Of course not. You would encourage the child to continue failing until the child learns to walk. The reward of walking is worth the failures."

Prospects and new distributors are worried that they might fail in our business. This prevents them from enrolling or even trying our business. I like to relieve their fears by letting them know that they can fail several times and still be successful.

I can't sponsor anyone.

"If there was a $50,000 cash reward for sponsoring six people in a week, you could do it. You will find in the long run that six first-level distributors are far more valuable than $50,000 cash. When you finally figure that out and believe it, you will have no trouble sponsoring."

I need to earn money right away.

"Figure on a six-month training period to learn our business. Where are you after six months in college? Still spending money on tuition. After six months in our business, you can actually be earning money instead of spending money on tuition for the next three-and-a-half years."

Make sure that you are clear on this. You are offering to **teach** them how to do your business in six months. You are not guaranteeing that they will be earning large checks in six months. They still have to work their business.

What if my good distributor quits?

"You can fail 19 out of 20 times when developing a leader. You only need one good leader to return your efforts with large bonus checks. This is much easier than the stock market where you have to be right almost 50% of the time."

It is a good thing that we aren't bankers. If a banker makes a couple of mistakes (bad loans), he's out of a job!

Getting your prospects to consider other possibilities in their lives.

"Are you married to your job or are you open-minded?"

This simple question almost always works. Most prospects feel that they are open-minded and agree to listen to a job alternative, a new view about health, changing services, etc.

I want to go full-time right away.

"Nothing magical happens when you quit your job - except that your income disappears."

--Art Spikol

I love this quote. When new distributors quit their jobs, they lose their warm market. Many of their initial sales and distributors will come from their full-time job contacts.

And it gets worse. Now that he is home during the day, the new distributor finds that he can't sponsor anyone because all of the prospects are at work. Since there isn't much to do, why not watch television? Aaaaack!

I am already successful.

"Lots of financially-successful people wish their unsuccessful friends could come with them on frequent cruises, vacations and holidays. But their friends can't. They have to work at their jobs.

"Unfortunately, many financially-successful people have special skills or knowledge that made them successful. Their friends can't duplicate their skills or knowledge. However, you might want to get involved in network marketing because this is something that your friends could successfully participate in. Now you can give them an opportunity that they can do.

"And wouldn't it be fun to have all your friends with you on your next vacation?"

Tired of your distributors blaming you for their lack of success?

Want to get your distributors to take personal responsibility for their success?

Simply slip this into your presentation while your negative distributors are listening:

"If you go out there and become a huge success in this business, it will not be because of me, it will be because of you.

"If you go out there and fail in this business, it will not be because of me, it will be because of you."

You are only one good prospect away from a $1,000,000 career!

Sometimes we get discouraged. That's human nature.

But we also have the **ability** to cheer ourselves up. Here is one way to create a positive outlook when we feel discouraged.

Just imagine that you continue promoting and talking about your network marketing business. At some point, you'll cross paths with a prospect that is looking for an opportunity to change his life — and you are the answer.

Maybe you don't know this prospect now. Maybe it will be a chance encounter sometime in the future. It doesn't matter how you meet this prospect. It just matters that you are still enthusiastic about your network marketing business and will impress your prospect.

What can one good prospect mean to you financially?

That one prospect could mean a million dollars over several years. And that's a powerful incentive to be persistent in your business.

There are many network marketing leaders today who enjoy powerful incomes because of just one good prospect.

Why not join them?

All you have to do is to stay in the game. Don't quit. And continue to promote your network marketing business.

Quick one-liners.

"The best thing we can do for the poor is to not be one of them."

"How many of us want our children to have rich parents?"

"Success isn't working at someone else's corporation."

Change how your distributors think about problems.

"I've got a problem. The company can't compete. Our prices are too high. I am a professional victim."

Sound familiar?

I often get calls from distributors who want their network marketing programs to be perfect, with perfect personnel, with perfect home office employees, with the lowest prices, with no competition, with no bad press, with ... well, you get the idea. They can't handle problems.

Since neither you nor I can fix all of their problems (and that wouldn't be much of a life if we tried), we must show our distributors how to turn problems into advantages.

How do you do this? Here are two quick generic case studies of how a bit of leadership and creative thinking can change how your distributors look at problems.

Case study #1: $5 Haircuts!

One barbershop offered $5 haircuts. His advertising was everywhere. The competing barbershop was losing business to the low-priced competitor.

To turn this disadvantage to his advantage, the more expensive barbershop placed this message in its advertising:

We fix $5 haircuts!

Since most people buy on quality, convenience, ease-of-use, etc., the higher-priced barbershop reclaimed lost business and thrived.

Case study #2: Gas guzzlers for sale.

When the first big oil crisis hit the United States in the 1970s, large, gas-guzzling automobile sales came to a halt. Everyone wanted to buy tiny, imported fuel-efficient automobiles.

Prospects wouldn't even go into a car dealership that sold those large, gas-guzzling automobiles. Here is what one dealership did to change the prospects' attitudes and buying criteria.

In front of his dealership he placed a tiny imported car that was crushed during a bad automobile accident. It was shocking. Prospects saw the damage the little car suffered and instantly thought about what could have happened to its passengers.

Now their buying criteria quickly changed from gas savings to **safety**.

Need some more examples?

Mud-tasting, awful coffee.

While traveling through a Canadian airport, I saw this sign outside a coffee shop:

"There is no strong coffee. Only weak men."

This coffee shop probably had a few complaints about its thick and strong coffee. So instead of looking at the complaints as a negative, the coffee shop turned the complaints into a "selling challenge."

Most men would now say:

"I only drink the real mud coffee from this coffee shop."

I don't think many men would come back to the coffee shop and say:

"Oooooohhh. This coffee is too strong for me. Do you have something wimpy like some hot tea and milk?"

The coffee shop has now turned its thick and strong coffee into an attraction for men. A man couldn't pass by the coffee shop and say:

"Oh, that looks too strong for me."

Gangs on street corners.

One city had trouble with gangs congregating on a certain street corner of the city. And yes, even this problem was addressed with just a little creative imagination.

The city's solution?

They started playing classical music in the area. And that was just too painful for the gangs to listen to. The corner became safe again.

Got the idea?

Every marketing problem can be improved by using some creative thinking. We can't solve every problem, but we can certainly make the problems less severe.

Now, let's have some examples for our business.

Imagine your city just landed the contract for the big automobile plant. Signs are everywhere that say:

"Now hiring! Good-paying jobs!"

Your distributors complain, "Nobody wants to come to the opportunity meetings. Nobody wants to start a part-time business. Everybody just wants to get one of those new, good-paying jobs at the automobile plant."

As a leader, you could recommend competing advertising that says:

"Lucky enough to miss out on that automobile job that would suck up the rest of your life? Have a career with us. Potential 5-day weekends!"

There will be plenty of prospects who don't want to sell five days out of every week to the automobile plant.

Or ...

Let's say that your vitamin product costs twice as much as the competition. You could say this:

"You could get a weaker product for about half the price, but you don't want to be only half-healthy, do you?"

Or if the taste of your health drink is bad, you could say:

"When you taste our drink, you will know it is healthy and good for you. You won't taste any sugar fillers that others use to dilute and weaken their drink."

Or if your skin care moisturizer is twice as expensive as your competition, you could say:

"You can have ordinary skin that eventually wrinkles and looks old, or you can use the best moisturizer in the world to keep your skin looking healthier and younger."

Or if your starting cost is $500 and your competition only charges $50, you could say:

"As you can see, this is a serious business that can help you earn a serious income. It is not a $50 gimmick that will leave you feeling cheated."

Use the above strategies.

So take a look at your business problems now. Is there a negative that you have been trying to hide from your distributors? Is there an objection that keeps your distributors' prospects from joining your business?

If you have negatives or problems, don't worry. You can turn them into great sales points with a little imagination.

As a leader, the next time your distributor calls with a problem, take a little time to educate him about this technique or you will be spending a lifetime attempting to fix unlimited problems. That wouldn't be fun.

Yes ... but ...

What if there was negative press about my problem? Wouldn't that make it difficult to talk to prospects?

Well, let's turn that negative press into positive sales and momentum.

Amateur distributors hate bad news. They hide under a brick, change their order line to an unlisted number, and change their last names. Not exactly the formula for increased sales, is it?

Perhaps you've had some bad news in your business. If you hate bad news, read on. Maybe you'll change your mind.

Have you ever heard the old saying by politicians about the press? It goes like this: "I don't care what they say about me, as long as they spell my name correctly."

In other words, any publicity (within reason) is good for their campaigns.

We're in direct marketing. Period. And in direct marketing we must have exposure, publicity, contacts. We can't let our opportunity or product be a secret.

If prospects don't know about us, never hear about us, can't find us ... well, you get the picture. We are roadkill. Our competition gets the exposure and sales, and we become like the typewriter repairman ... very, very, very lonely.

Does this sound familiar? Maybe you've heard it worded another way, such as when our distributors say, "I don't have anybody to talk to."

Ever heard that? That means their direct marketing stinks. They are a secret. They are lonely. They are a failure. They are going to quit shortly ... and **you** better start doing something about it.

Okay, okay. We need some exposure out there to get more recruiting and retailing activity. Let's allow the bad news to help us. How? By turning bad news into a selling and recruiting opportunity. That is what the marketing pros do. So why don't we?

Let's use some examples.

Example #1.

The Attorney General says, "The Wonderful Company is an illegal pyramid!"

That's the headline of your local newspaper.

Ouch!

But now you are on the map. People know about you. Bringing up the Wonderful Company name in conversation guarantees that people will listen. Yes, we are celebrities now!

What can we do with our new-found popularity? How about a little retailing?

Imagine you're standing around the water cooler with a few co-workers. One co-worker says, "Did you read the paper this morning? The government says that the Wonderful Company is a rip-off pyramid scheme that sacrifices toads and unicorns in secret midnight opportunity meetings. Their two-headed alien president is believed to be responsible for World War II, the failure of the 1969 Chicago Cubs, and our recent increase in cigarette prices."

Everyone nods.

Then you say, "Yeah, I read that too. I am one of their best distributors. But last night I missed the big anniversary sacrifices at the cemetery. The Simpsons were on TV."

Whoa! Now we have their attention! (And isn't "attention" the first step in the selling process?) Then we continue by saying:

"Just kidding. You know you can't believe everything the government tells us. They want us to believe the IRS just wants to help us, that raising their salaries and our taxes at the same time is just a coincidence, and that planting a computer chip in our heads is just to make sure we don't get lost going home at night."

Everyone smiles. They know you are right. They know the newspaper regularly reports Elvis sightings. They know you can't trust the government. You are building trust and rapport. And you continue:

"I think the government and a few big lobbyists are upset that we sell the Wonderful Arthritis Pain Killer for only $25. That means a lot of doctors, pharmacists, big drug companies and politicians aren't getting their profits and kickbacks. I mean, when the public finds out they don't have to pay big bucks for doctor visits and expensive drugs and shots, somebody in the government is going to be red-faced with embarrassment. My next door neighbor spends $25 a month on the Wonderful Arthritis Pain Killer and is now playing tennis. I bet she laughed when she saw this morning's paper." (Looks like we had a chance here to slip in some facts and benefits.)

A fellow worker replies, "Yeah, it is a big conspiracy up there at the Capitol. They are always trying to soak us little guys. Say, do you happen to have an extra bottle for my mother-in-law? She is always complaining about this and that."

Hmmmm. Now what do we think about this morning's newspaper headline? Was it bad news ... or an opportunity for sales?

The bad news gave us an opportunity to talk about our product without coming up to a cold prospect and saying: "Hey there, looks like you're limping, buddy. Try my Wonderful Arthritis Pain Killer for 30 days. It's only $25 retail."

What's wrong with coming up to cold prospects? Well, they don't know us, they don't trust us, and they don't know anything about our company or product. Just about everything is wrong. As direct marketers, we don't want to be cold-calling salesmen or peddlers. That is why we welcome news about our company and our products and opportunity. Even if it is bad news.

Example #2.

The local TV station announces that carrot powder is now a dangerous, restricted drug and that dieters should return their bottles of carrot powder for a refund.

It is getting easier already, isn't it? This one is simple.

While standing around the donut shop, your friends say, "Don't you sell carrot powder? Didn't the news say something last night about a recall?" Just the conversation you were waiting to hear. You reply:

"Yep. They are recalling carrot powder off the shelves. Seems that while a few thousand folks lost a lot of weight, a couple of people got upset stomachs. Too bad. By the way, do you know of anybody who is presently taking carrot powder or other diet products?"

One friend replies, "Sure do. All my brothers are taking carrot powder. Boy, they need it too. Those boys are fat. The big grocery companies even offered to build a chain of stores around them."

Now, you've just located some prospects in a round-about, referral sort of way. You say:

"Great. Did you know they can return their carrot powder for a 100% refund and get the new 'Rippling Muscle Diet Herbs' at half-price during the next seven days?"

Your friend replies, "Really? Where can they get the refunds? How does it work?" (Do I need to go on from here? Get the picture?)

You answer, "Just give me their phone numbers. I will call them with all the details. In fact, I can take care of the whole thing for them."

What we are experiencing is:

1. Bad news = publicity.

2. Publicity = prospects.

3. Prospects + knowledge = an opportunity to sell more products.

Example #3.

Direct marketing expert Mike Enlow wrote a newsletter and used the Internet extensively for marketing. His website advertised his products, provided visitors with information, etc.

Now, one way that Mike let people know about his site was to place messages in different newsgroups and forums. **Unfortunately**, many Internet sites hate advertisements and press releases. They only want news or "non-commercial" type discussions. Mike's posting of messages to advertise his site would be a serious public relations mistake.

With no way of getting publicity to advertise your services, what do you do?

You hope for some bad news.

Here is what happened to Mike Enlow. A computer hacker trashed his Web site by uploading and overloading his site with junk. This effectively put his site out of service for the day. Bad news? Sure. But look what Mike did with the bad news.

Mike knew that the most Internet sites hated advertising, but always welcomed news, requests for help, discussions, etc. He posted a message on these Internet sites that said:

"My name is Mike Enlow. My Internet site was trashed by hackers. Took a day to put it back together. All of the good free information I offered was unavailable to the public because of some unknown computer hacker. I am offering a $10,000 reward for the identity of this hacker."

Actually the message was longer, but you get the general idea.

What happened? People reading this on the Internet rushed to Mike Enlow's website to see what it was all about. Lots of activity and new users. And no one collected the $10,000. However, this announcement might have been more potent than any advertising message.

Bad news? Or, was it good news? You be the judge.

Example #4.

You mail a monthly newsletter to your downline. It is called *Smith's Universal Successful Journal*. Your name is Smith and you want to think positive, so you think *Smith's Universal Successful Journal* is a good name.

Now imagine there is a large commercial publication called *Successful Journal*. The overpaid attorneys at *Successful Journal* say, "Hey, this *Smith's Universal Successful Journal* newsletter sounds a little bit too much like our trademarked title of *Successful Journal*. Let's sue Ms. Smith."

Bad news. A real David and Goliath saga begins. Mega-big *Successful Journal* sues Ms. Smith to make her change the name of her 100-name circulation newsletter.

Or, is it good news?

The newspaper writes a story about how Ms. Smith's newsletter gave friendly recipes on low-fat foods and told its readers about food supplementation and weight-loss tips. Over 40,000 readers see this story.

The local radio station interviews Ms. Smith. She carefully explains to the listeners, "My newsletter is just to help people feel better, live a little longer, and lose up to 15 pounds of ugly fat a month. I certainly didn't feel I was infringing upon the *Successful Journal* trademark. So, I want to take this opportunity to make it perfectly clear, I am not the *Successful Journal*. I write the newsletter that helps people lose weight. Not the newsstand *Successful Journal*. I am the one who gives free $10 certificates for Super-Weight-Off."

The bad news is beginning to look pretty good now, isn't it? Even if Ms. Smith changes the name of her newsletter, she still gains thousands of dollars in free publicity.

So that's the technique.

Bad news isn't so bad after all. What should professional marketers do when bad news come?

They should use the publicity as an excuse to contact present customers and new prospects. Maybe you should go out and create a little bad news today.

The only free cheese is in the mousetrap.

What do network marketing leaders know that struggling, unsuccessful distributors don't know?

What is the real inside secret that leaders use to become successful?

Why do some distributors join company after company and never succeed in any company?

The answer is ...

Network marketing leaders know that "making it happen" is up to them.

They can't depend on their sponsor, their sponsor's sponsor, or their network marketing company to build their business for them. If leaders are going to have a profitable business, they must build it themselves.

- Network marketing leaders know that it is always too early to quit.
- Network marketing leaders know that you lead by personal example.

- Network marketing leaders know that successful people perform the activities that unsuccessful people shun.
- Network marketing leaders know that no one is going to build a business for them.
- Network marketing leaders know that you must first dig a foundation before you can build your castle.

So what about those unsuccessful distributors that go from company to company, new downline to new downline, always looking for success?

They are looking in the **wrong place** for success.

Success comes from **personal** effort, not from handouts by strangers.

What do unsuccessful distributors do?

- They complain that the products are too expensive.
- They complain that the literature and product labels are all the wrong color.
- They complain that their upline has done nothing for them — yet they have done nothing themselves.
- They complain they have no upline support — so they constantly look for a sponsor who will do all the work for them!!!

Hmmm, maybe that is why they switch from company to company.

They are always looking for a new sponsor who might do their work for them.

Does this typical phone call sound familiar?

Distributor: Hello? Glad I caught you. I need some help.

Sponsor: What can I do?

Distributor: This business isn't growing fast enough. There is something wrong with the company. I'm just not making any money.

Sponsor: Any business worth having is going to take time and effort. Why not stick with me? We'll just work a little harder, and let's see what happens.

Distributor: No, I'm going to have to quit and go to a company where I can earn some real money. I've worked this business hard for 60 days and I still haven't earned a bonus check over $50! You call this a financial opportunity? HA!

Sponsor: Have you recruited anybody this week?

Distributor: No. I am just not making enough money.

Sponsor: Have you made any appointments this week?

Distributor: No. This business is just not paying off. I'm not getting any new growth in my downline.

Sponsor: Have you done any prospecting in the last four weeks?

Distributor: No. Of course not. This business just isn't growing like it should. Besides, I just heard of a new company where people are making really big money. And the guy signing me up is a real heavy hitter.

Sponsor: And this heavy hitter is going to prospect, sign up new distributors, put them in your group, retail, and do all the work for you, and ... let you have all the money, right?

Distributor: Uh yeah, I guess so. Say, I must be going now. I'll catch you another time. Bye.

Pay me more than I am worth.

Or, have you had a distributor that sabotages his efforts and thinks like this?

This distributor wants to become a leader and make at least $10,000 a month.

And, he insists that he should already be earning $10,000 a month after just six months with your company. After all, the company can't be any good if you can't earn at least $10,000 a month after six months of part-time work.

You ask your distributor, "How much do you earn in your present job that you've been working for the past 12 years?"

He replies, "About $3,000 a month."

Does he get the hint? No.

So then you ask your distributor how much sales volume he moved in his organization last month.

He replies, "My group moves $5,000 in products every month!"

Weird. Your distributor still thinks he should earn $10,000 a month, even though he provides far less than $10,000 a month in value to your company.

You can predict your distributor's future. He will insist that it is the company's fault and he will just have to look for another opportunity that will pay him $10,000 a month after six months' work. It doesn't matter if he provides very little value and service, he just deserves $10,000 a month.

A story to remember.

I got this "non-leadership" story from Ben Woodward in England:

A 38-year-old man was at his parents' home for Sunday dinner. He mournfully turned the discussion to his many problems. He whimpered to his parents:

"I've just left my third failed marriage, I can't hold on to a job, I'm in debt up to my ears and will have to declare personal bankruptcy. Where did **you** go wrong?"

How to challenge your distributors to take personal responsibility and think like leaders.

I love the following story:

The president of a network marking company had just created a "Miracle Product." This product cured almost every health problem imaginable.

At the company convention, the president asked for volunteers to come to the stage.

To the first distributor volunteer, the president said, "What health problem do you have?"

The distributor answered, "My vision. Each year I need stronger and stronger glasses. I am now blind in one eye and I can barely see out of the other eye."

The president gave a drink of "Miracle Product" to the distributor. Instantly the distributor threw off his glasses and proclaimed, "I can see! I can see! My vision is perfect!"

The president turned to the second distributor volunteer and said, "What health problem do you have?"

The second distributor answered, "My arthritis. I can barely bend one knee and I have to drag my other leg behind me."

The president gave a drink of "Miracle Product" to the second distributor. Instantly the distributor volunteer threw away his crutches, jumped into the air, and then cartwheeled off the stage while yelling, "I am cured! I am cured!"

The third volunteer on stage was the worthless sponsor. Upon seeing the miracle cures, the worthless sponsor started running away while yelling, "Don't you come near me! Don't touch me! I am still collecting disability!"

Hey! Look here! It's not crowded at the top.

Network marketing success comes from personal effort. That is too bad for the "free cheese" seekers. However, this does makes life pleasant and uncrowded at the top.

Or, as Dolly Parton said,

"The way I see it, if you want the rainbow, you gotta put up with the rain."

Free cheese is tempting.

Professional television spectators want the free cheese. Couch potatoes want the free cheese. And yes, lazy distributors want the free cheese.

But if handouts were really free, don't you think that hard-working, aggressive network marketing leaders would get the free cheese **before** the lazy freeloaders of life?

Events are neutral.

"It doesn't matter what happens. It is how you react to what happens that determines your success."

Do your distributors become discouraged every time your network marketing company changes policies, increases shipping charges, or adjusts the compensation plan? What should you do?

Replace your negative-thinking group? Reprogram the home office? Get a job with the government?

Don't do anything rash yet. First, let's look at the cause, not the symptoms.

Most things that happen are called **events. Events**, by their very nature, are **neutral**. That is, the event is neither good nor bad.

It is our reaction to an event that can be good or bad.

Your new distributors haven't reached the maturity level in their careers where they realize that they are in control of their reactions — the same reactions that can make an event good or bad.

So much for the philosophy.

Let's use a few examples to show how events are neutral and our reactions **determine** if we feel good or bad about the event.

Imagine your city's team is playing in the World Series. Final game. Last inning. Your favorite player hits a home run and your team wins. Now, that is an event!

Now, I ask you, was that event good, bad, or neutral?

As a loyal fan of your hometown team, you reacted to the event with a happy, positive feeling of excitement. You might have hugged your spouse, called your bookie to collect your winnings, and given a generous pledge to a local charity — or something like that.

If you were a fan of the losing team, you might have reacted to the event with violent, negative, childish passion. You might have pounded your fist on the coffee table, thrown a gum wrapper on the floor, or even yelled some things that we can't print. Yes, your reaction to the event (the winning home run) was negative.

Now, we have two opposite reactions to the event. One is positive, the other is negative. So, now what is your answer?

The actual event was neutral.

The positive and negative reactions are all caused by individual interpretations. And that is something we, as responsible adults, can handle.

Let's use another example. Imagine that your company raised prices on your most popular product. Is that **event** positive, negative, or neutral?

It is neutral. We can personally choose to take a positive or a negative position. That is our choice, but the **event** remains neutral.

You could say,

"Oh, my! This is terrible! Our Wonder Product now costs $2.50 more to the retail customer. No one can afford it. The company is too greedy. Life is unfair. The world is trying to sabotage my business, etc., etc., etc."

I'm sure you could fill in some more here, but let's get on to a different reaction. You could also react to that **event** by saying,

"Wow! That's great! Looks like the company is keeping up with inflation and rising costs. Pretty good financial managers there. Looks like we will be in business for the long run with that kind of leadership. Plus, they might have improved the quality or added ingredients. Hey, with the price increase, I will be earning more commissions and bonuses on each sale. This price increase is terrific!"

Again, the **event** (the price increase) is neutral. It is how one chooses to react to the **event** that makes a difference.

For our last **event** example, let's imagine that your sponsor's telephone is no longer in service. Is that an **event**? Sure. Is that a neutral **event**? Let's see.

You could say,

"That jerk! My sponsor can't even manage his finances well enough to pay his own phone bill. How am I supposed to do three-way calls with my sponsor? What does he expect me to do? Stay at home and wait for his calls from a phone booth to give me company update information? What a disaster!"

Or, you could react to the event by saying,

"Great! Now I can get some real work done. I won't be tied up on the phone with that jerk anymore. Now I can give my own opportunity meetings. And, while my sponsor is incognito, I can go out and sponsor some great people without his competition. Yeah! Keep that phone disconnected!"

So, what about your downline members who choose to have a negative reaction to every event?

Why not take the time to educate your downline and show them that they have a choice? They can react positively or negatively to the **event** — the choice is strictly up to them.

Once your new distributors realize that they control the reactions to **events**, your worries are over. They can **no longer** say,

"Oh, this **event** is bad so I am going to quit, join another opportunity, or go to work for the postal service. These other opportunities have better **events**."

They can't say that because they know that **events** are everywhere, they are happening all the time and that **events** will occur no matter where they go in life.

You don't become successful because of **neutral events**. You become successful because of your **reaction** to these **neutral events**.

Teaching "activity thinking" to distributors.

If you are not happy with your bonus check …

Take **action** … and then comes the result.

Every action or activity will produce a result. If you don't like the result, simply change the action.

For instance, hit your hand with a hammer.

Ouch! That really hurts.

Now, hit your hand with a hammer again.

Ouch! That really hurts.

Now, hit your hand with a hammer again.

Ouch! Ouch! Ouch! That really, really hurts.

Get the picture?

First you perform an action or activity (hitting your hand with a hammer.)

Then you'll get a predictable result from that activity (Ouch! Ouch! Ouch!)

If you want different results, simply change your activity.

How?

Try hitting your friend's hand with a hammer. (Result: now your friend says, "Ouch, ouch!")

Let's try this principle again.

Today you get into your automobile and commute two hours to work. You arrive at the job, get paid peanuts, and you hate every minute you are there.

Tomorrow you get into your automobile and commute two hours to work. You arrive at the job, get paid peanuts, and you hate every minute you are there.

Hmmm, I bet if you get into your automobile tomorrow and commute two hours to work — you just might arrive at the job, get paid peanuts, and hate every minute you are there.

Same activity — same results.

If you want different results, simply change your activity.

How?

Drive to the golf course, to a trade school, to a new job interview. If you don't like the results you are getting, simply change your activity.

Sure makes sense, doesn't it?

Why doesn't everyone see this?

Go down to the local bar and listen to the patrons complain.

They'll say,

"Man, I can't stand my job. Every day it is the same old thing. And my boss is a jerk! The pay is lousy. The traffic is killing me and I can't get a week off when I want."

You feel like saying to them,

"Maybe if you drove somewhere else every morning, you wouldn't end up at the job you hate, and the boss you hate."

Of course, free advice such as this can be hazardous to your health.

It is frustrating to see this activity/results concept clearly.

Why?

Because we know there is a solution to almost every complaint, and the rest of the world doesn't see a thing.

Does this happen in network marketing?

Sure. Did you ever hear this statement?

"I just can't find any prospects."

Your distributor complains,

"I can't be successful because I just can't find any prospects. It is my upline's fault, the company's fault, the product's fault, I live too far away from meetings, I don't know anyone. Nobody likes me. The weather is lousy. And I have to work on weekdays!"

Well, maybe all these **are** legitimate complaints.

So what?

Complaining won't make any of those problems go away. Repeating these problems to you won't make the weather better or make the distributor's house magically move closer to the meetings.

Your complaining distributor will just have to realize:

"If you don't like the results, simply change the activity."

All this cause-and-effect stuff isn't that complicated. Let's apply some of it to your distributor's problems.

Problem: "I have to work on weekdays!"

Activity change: Get a night job instead. Work weekends. Get a job working from home. Win the lottery. Have your spouse get a higher-paying job. Take early retirement.

See the difference? Your distributor must take personal responsibility for his actions and be willing to change the activity. When the activity changes, so do the results. Let's look at the next problem.

Problem: "The weather is lousy."

Activity change: Move to a better climate. Buy a raincoat. Stay inside.

Problem: "Nobody likes me."

Activity change: Learn to smile. Take a self-improvement course. Meet new people who don't know you.

Problem: "I don't know anyone."

Activity change: Meet new people. Go to a party. Join a community organization. Advertise. Do mailings. Start a Facebook account. Do volunteer work.

Problem: "I don't know what to say to prospects over the telephone."

Activity change: Attend Saturday morning trainings. Read a book on telephone techniques. Listen to telephone training audios.

Will this "activity thinking" change my business?

Only if your distributors accept this new way of thinking about their problems. We will have to do plenty of examples over time before their beliefs change to personal responsibility. But "activity thinking" will move them closer to leadership.

Why personal growth and skill development are critical.

You hear your sponsor say:

"Listen to these personal growth audios. Read these personal growth books. Learn new skills. Go to this seminar. Take this attitude course."

But why?

Certainly it will make you a better person, but here is why I think it is so important.

New prospects will be attracted to you.

Prospects are attracted to people who have information they want.

Imagine there are three women at a party.

One woman is a doctor. She is surrounded by people who are asking her to suggest a treatment, to look at their mole, to recommend something for their sickly child, etc. The doctor has information they want. They are **attracted** to her.

The second woman is a realtor. She is surrounded by people who are asking her which neighborhood is appreciating, how much their house is worth, or where they can get good financing. The realtor has information they want. They are **attracted** to her.

The third woman is complaining that her children never visit her, the potholes on her street are getting bigger, her favorite talk show comes on too early in the afternoon, and that she has constant aches and pains. No one is around this lady. She doesn't have any information that other people want. **No one** is attracted to her.

In a "prospect-meets-distributor" situation, the prospects make a **quick decision** whether or not you **have** information that they want. If you don't, you are going to be very lonely.

You have to have something to offer to your prospects.

And here is where it gets very interesting.

Most new distributors try to get prospects by **giving** gifts, sending them free stuff, or inviting them to dinner or lunch. This will make prospects like them because they are nice. But being nice seldom leads to **attraction**.

Attraction comes from having the **information** your prospects desire to improve their lives. That is why we try to learn as much as we can through personal development. Now it makes sense.

So wouldn't now be a good time to learn more about prospecting, building a business, how the mind works, tax strategies, marketing, and leadership?

People are desperate to learn these things to improve their lives. Will they be **attracted** to you because you have this **information**? Or will you have nothing to offer?

A dirty, little-known secret in network marketing.

As leaders, we need to educate our distributors and potential leaders. If we don't, they will use the wrong strategies to build their business.

For example, they will desperately search for the **perfect prospect** that will make them rich.

That is probably a waste of time.

You see, even if a networker found the perfect prospect, would the perfect prospect be interested in this networker?

Would this perfect prospect be willing to follow a networker who was **dependent** on finding someone else to become successful?

Of course not.

Great prospects are **attracted** to great people.

The attraction test.

Imagine that you are walking down a city street in an abandoned warehouse district. It is dark. It is deserted. You pass a man lying in the gutter. He has three empty bottles of wine beside him. His clothes are grimy. He hasn't shaved. And, he is talking rather loudly to himself.

Would you move to the other side of the sidewalk as you passed him?

What would you do if he offered you his business card and invited you to an opportunity meeting?

Would you take him seriously? Probably not.

You wouldn't be rejecting the opportunity. You would be rejecting **the person** and this encounter.

Now, imagine that you saw George Washington, the first president of the United States, standing on the corner just a little farther down the street. As you passed him, George says,

"Here is my card and a brochure about a great business opportunity. If you like what you see, give me a call and we will get together for lunch."

Your thoughts?

"Wow! If George has given up politics for this business opportunity, I had better check it out. I bet he is marketing some secret food supplement that makes you live to be 300 years old."

See the difference?

George and the drunk in the gutter are distributors for the **same** network marketing company.

You pay attention to George. You are attracted to George. You perceive George as someone with skills and knowledge that could help you succeed.

In other words, you respect George Washington and will **consider** his invitation while you would **ignore** the invitation from the drunk in the gutter.

Success is **in** George — not outside of George. And just think of all the knowledge that George could pass on to you with his centuries of hands-on experience.

Are you getting any ideas how you, your distributors, and your potential leaders could **become more valuable** for your network marketing prospects?

What if you became a network marketing tax expert? You would attract prospects who wanted a part-time business to increase their possible deductions.

What if you read and studied to become a motivational expert? You would **attract** prospects looking for positive energy to fill their lives.

What if you became a product expert? You would **attract** prospects who wanted to know how your products could improve the quality of their lives.

What if you became a marketing expert? A retailing expert?

A prospecting expert? A training expert?

The real key to networking is becoming a better you.

People seek knowledge, guidance, motivation, understanding, and more. Where will they go to get it?

- Not to the drunk in the gutter.
- Not to the so-called leader who quit because of a shipping problem.
- Not to the person who stopped learning when he left school.
- And certainly not to the person who believes he has reached the apex of his potential.

I'm okay and I don't need to get any better.

You wouldn't buy a computer from a company that announces,

"This is the best computer we can make. We will never be able to build a better model."

You wouldn't buy a car from GM or Ford if they declared,

"We will never improve on this model. We are stopping our research today."

And, you wouldn't sponsor under a network marketing distributor who said,

"I don't need any more knowledge or improvement. I am set for life. Any new knowledge will have to be ignored. I can't improve myself."

Well, unsuccessful distributors don't actually say it that way, but you pick up the signals pretty easily.

The unsuccessful distributor doesn't go to meetings, doesn't attend trainings, doesn't read new books, doesn't listen to educational audios, and limits his exposure to new information from late-night cable television infomercials.

Is this the person you want for a sponsor?

Is this the person you want to lead you to success? Of course not.

This person believes success is **outside** of him. This person is hoping that you or some other prospect will make him successful!

These phone calls tell the real story.

Don't take my word for it.

Do what I did. I called a few network marketing leaders and asked them what they learned last week. Here are their answers:

Leader #1: "I am reading *The Richest Man in Babylon.* I have noticed that some of the long-time networkers who made a lot of money … well, they are broke. I don't want to be like them. I want to manage my bonus checks wisely and invest for my financial future. Plus, I listened to some marketing audios all this week while I was driving."

Leader #2: "I just came back from a direct marketing seminar. It wasn't specifically for network marketing, but it gave me a broader view of how I will develop a recruiting campaign for my downline. Plus, on the plane, I finished reading a book on making new friends."

Leader #3: "I flew to the company convention. I learned a lot of tips from my fellow leaders and I'm including them in my monthly training meeting with my downline. I also listened to sales training audios by Tom Hopkins and Frank Bettger."

It's not hard to pick up the pattern here. These are networking leaders because they constantly improve themselves.

Now, what did my phone calls to unsuccessful distributors reveal?

Unsuccessful distributor #1: "I just don't have time to get to the monthly company training seminars. By the time my softball league finishes in the evening, I don't have the energy. I am still looking for some good distributors, but haven't found any lately."

Unsuccessful distributor #2: "I really don't like reading. Never did. No, I don't know how our bonus plan works. And, I do have trouble giving a presentation, so I haven't done any. I am not sure this networking business really works. I haven't seen any bonus checks yet."

Unsuccessful distributor #3: "Every week it is the same old opportunity meeting. Never changes. It is too boring to keep going there — especially when I don't have any guests or prospects."

It is not too hard to detect a trend here.

Is there a time when you can stop learning and improving?

You would have to ask someone a lot older than I am.

I took an inventory of just the books I've read recently as part of my personal self-improvement campaign.

First, I read *Ogilvy on Advertising*. Why? I figured he knew more about how to reach customers' minds than anyone else during the last 40 years.

I re-read *The Five Great Rules of Selling* by Percy Whiting. This book shows how selling was done in the 1950s and 1960s. It's great to compare to how it is done today.

I read about 60 pages from *Dartnell's Direct Mail and Mail Order Handbook*. (I am pacing myself ... this book is 1,538 pages long.)

I read a bit of *A Brief History of Time* by Stephen Hawking. A humbling experience. A bit over my head, so I think I will just rent the video.

And finally, I read *The Far Side Gallery 2* for a little light reading. Of course I read this volume cover-to-cover since cartoons are addictive.

Why so much reading? Because I prefer reading to audios. But for many, it will be just the opposite.

Do leaders go to training seminars? Sure.

Do leaders seek out people with knowledge and expertise who will help with their business? You bet! They love taking experts to lunch.

The bottom line?

You must give people a **reason** to **want** you as their sponsor. You want prospects to seek you out, to look for you as their trusted mentor. You want prospects to be excited to join your team.

So, all you have to do is remember:

The ultimate secret to successful sponsoring is not finding the right person, but being the right person.

Life in network marketing gets a lot easier when people are attracted to you.

Do you think that's why it seems that the leaders get all the good prospects?

Don't send your new distributors on a fatal leap into the unknown.

An insurance salesman spends $500 on an airline ticket to see a prospect. A car salesman spends $400 in a national trade publication to find potential purchasers. A dry cleaner rents a $350 meeting room and runs an opportunity meeting for his dry cleaning services. A drugstore clerk rents 500 names and telephone numbers of strangers from throughout the United States and cold-calls them to see if they want toiletries and skin care products.

Strange? I think so.

As professional network marketers, we would **laugh** at these desperate and expensive attempts to create new business. Yet sometimes we tolerate this shameful waste of money by new distributors in our group.

Think about it. A new distributor has these **natural advantages** when talking to his warm market:

- The prospect knows the distributor and probably likes him.
- It is easier to get an appointment with someone you know.

- A face-to-face presentation involves all of the senses. The prospect can touch and see the products and services.

If our new distributor is unable to sponsor a warm market prospect with all of these built-in advantages, how could we possibly expect our distributor to be successful with strangers? The new distributor would have to overcome these challenges with strangers:

- The prospect is skeptical of an unsolicited phone call from a stranger.
- The prospect wants to watch television and finish dinner instead of listening to a telephone presentation.
- The prospect can't see, touch or feel the products or services.
- There is no natural bond or relationship with a stranger.

The bottom line is that if a new distributor **doesn't have the skills** to sponsor warm market contacts, going to the cold market is going to be ugly.

As responsible upline leaders, we should recognize the real problem here – **lack of skills**.

Instead of allowing our new distributors to waste money locating new prospects (that they will successfully discourage from joining their businesses), let's help our new distributors invest the time and money to learn the skills necessary to sponsor prospects successfully.

- Why not teach your new distributor the right phrases to say, and what not to say?

- Why not encourage your new distributors to invest a few hours at your "Get Started" training?

I am sure you or someone in your upline has some type of training to make it easier for new distributors. In a few hours you could help them build a confident belief in the products and services and teach them some basic presentation skills.

When your new distributors become confident, amazing things happen. Their prospects have more confidence in them.

Remember, if your new distributor can't sponsor a close friend face-to-face, sponsoring complete strangers by telephone or the Internet is going to be ugly.

Invest in yourself.

It is claimed that Henry Ford said:

"Invest 10% of your income in yourself, in learning and training, to become a better person. Continue to invest 10% until age 40. Instead of investing in securities or real estate, invest in yourself, **it's a better return**. Then, at age 40 start investing in securities or real estate because then you will have more money."

Or, as I like to say:

"Invest in yourself unless you feel it would be a poor investment."

The best money hedge or inflation hedge is not gold, real estate or stocks. The safest hedge is investing in yourself.

One day a leader called me and said:

"Hey, I have $5,000 to invest. Maybe I should invest it in a hot growth stock. Wouldn't that be a good investment? And maybe I can get a great return."

My answer was:

"It's nice that you want to invest in a hot growth stock. I can't really predict if the stock price will go up or down. However, let's say that it goes up. Amazingly you purchase the stock at the perfect time, and your stock goes up 40% over the next 12 months. Wow! What a return. That means your $5,000 investment is now worth $7,000 with your 40% increase. Can't argue with that. That is a good return.

"However, what if you invested the same $5,000 in your business? Maybe you drove across the country and visited your top groups. While giving a meeting, you touched just one person who joined because of your message. That person became a leader and earned you $1,000 a month, every month ... **for the rest of your life**! Now that would be an awesome return on your investment.

"Or, maybe you invested in some training for your serious workers and leaders. Because they now look upon you as a partner instead of just an upline sponsor collecting checks, they work harder. And, they work harder with the new skills they learned in training. Your group **doubles** its volume and your bonus check **doubles**. Wow. That would be a spectacular return on your investment.

"Or, you run a series of ads looking for people dissatisfied with their careers and willing to invest one or two years into learning how to build a networking business. Your ads attract three new leaders who are anxious to build their businesses. That would be a huge return on your investment every month.

"Which would you rather have in your business? A one-time extra $2,000 return on your $5,000 investment from a good stock pick, or would you rather have three new leaders building their business?"

The choice is easy. **Invest in yourself** and in your business because you can get a better return on your investment.

There is nothing wrong with stocks, bonds, and real estate. We are simply looking for the best return on our investment. So …

"Invest in yourself unless you feel it would be a poor investment."

Getting more results with your limited time.

When your distributors call, what do you do?

- Do you listen intently as they tell you their problems?
- Do you patiently listen to their personal dramas?
- Are you constantly being asked to do their work for them?
- Do they make you feel **responsible** for the failures in their lives and in their businesses?
- Do they waste your time with endless stories of past events and problems?

If this sounds familiar, why not be a bit more proactive? Why not have a strategy that will lead them to be more responsible in their lives?

Here are some of my favorite proactive responses:

"What would a leader do in this situation?"

Deborah Kay from Canada gave me this response. When distributors call her with problems, this is her favorite comeback.

Notice that she doesn't say that one has to be a leader. She only asks what a leader would do. They don't have to be a leader, and they don't have to take their own advice, but this does force them to come up with a responsible solution.

And, it makes them feel a little bit guilty about not appearing to be a leader by complaining.

"How long should your period of mourning be?"

Do you ever have distributors who are still blaming their failures on some past event? For example, their previous company went out of business two years ago, but they insist that the experience prevents them from recruiting.

I have a friend who got divorced six years ago, and still hasn't got over it. The divorce shows up in almost every whining session. You have to think,

"How long should your period of mourning be?"

People will hold onto past traumas forever unless you do something. Shock them out of using the past as an excuse for today. Make them commit to mourning a certain period of time, and then never bringing up that issue again.

"Fish eat when they are hungry, not when you drop the line."

Makes sense, doesn't it?

However, distributors believe that when they run a big prospecting campaign, everyone they contact should be looking for an opportunity at that moment.

It doesn't work that way.

No matter how good your brochure is, some people won't be hungry for an opportunity.

For example, maybe your business just came out with the super bonus program. You think everyone should join now. You approach a young lady and insist that she comes to tonight's opportunity meeting. She says:

"Oh, I don't think I can come. I am getting married this afternoon, and then there is the reception this evening. And I don't think I will want to set an appointment for a few weeks since we are leaving for our honeymoon tomorrow."

Accept the fact that not everyone is hungry for an opportunity at the exact moment you contact them.

So if your distributors complain that no one came to their opportunity meeting, simply explain that people only come when the time is right for them, not when the time is right for your distributors.

"What would you like me to do that you are unwilling to do yourself?"

You know how this conversation goes. The distributors call and constantly ask for help. They want you to prospect for them, do the presentation, enroll the new prospect, and then to notify them by email that you have helped them.

Everything is too hard for them to do. They have no time, no money, no skills, and you owe it to them to do their work for them. Ouch.

I won't say that the above phrase stops all of this nonsense, but it does help. Plus, I really like to say it.

This phrase will certainly reduce the requests for you to find perfect prospects that are ready to join, and hand-deliver them to your lazy distributor.

"What are the last five books you have read to improve your business?"

When distributors whine that they don't know what to do, this is an appropriate comeback to put the responsibility back on them. Sure, we want to meet distributors halfway, but they want us to do everything for them, including the thinking.

When you ask for the list of the last five books that they have read, most distributors realize that they haven't put much effort in their business. It is easy for them to ask you:

"Just tell me what to do that is guaranteed, rejection-free, takes no time, and is easy. And, I want it to work for everyone I meet."

Distributors don't have the right to ask you this question if they haven't tried to learn anything on their own. Make them at least try to learn. Don't read their books for them, or listen to their training audios for them.

Consider this strategy:

You don't have to do all the work for your downline.

You know the scenario. You are having dinner with your family and the telephone rings. The caller says:

"Hey, upline. My business isn't doing so well. What are you going to do about it?"

Everyone who fails wants to make it somebody else's fault or responsibility. If a distributor's business is failing, who is really to blame?

Is the upline to blame?

Take an average sponsor who has been in the business for five years. Some of the distributors he sponsored are successful. Some of the distributors he sponsored are unsuccessful.

Yet, both the successful distributors and the unsuccessful distributors have the **exact same sponsor!**

Take a lousy sponsor who has been in the business for five years. Some of the distributors he sponsored are successful. Some of the distributors he sponsored are unsuccessful.

Yet, both these successful distributors and these unsuccessful distributors have the **exact same sponsor!**

So, you can't blame the sponsor. The responsibility for success lies entirely with the distributor.

If you tell a distributor he failed because of his actions, that seems a little harsh. After all, if the distributor understood that he was entirely responsible for his success, well, he would probably already be a success.

So, how do you help your unsuccessful distributor focus on the real cause of his failure, his actions?

Well, go back to Volume One in this Leadership series, and start methodically, step-by-step, teaching this distributor how to think. But, **only** do that if this distributor passes the leadership test from Volume One.

What's more likely is that you will want to find someone who is already a bit further along in understanding personal responsibility. So where can you find someone new?

Read on.

"Are we looking for leaders in all the wrong places?"

I was speaking on the annual MLM cruise. About 40 people were in this session. All 40 were leaders.

How did I know they were leaders?

Well, they had a choice of lounging in the sun or learning new techniques to build their businesses. The leaders chose to attend this session. It is really easy to know who the leaders are.

During the session I asked the question:

"How were you introduced to network marketing?"

This is an important question. If we can find where leaders come from ... aha! We know where we can go to get more leaders.

Simple logic, right?

I gave the group of 40 leaders some choices to answer my question.

Here are the choices:

A. Relative or friend

B. Newspaper advertising

C. A mailing

D. An audio or CD

E. At a trade show

F. Radio advertising

G. The Internet

H. By referral

I. By a stranger at a chance encounter

J. Saw a flyer

Ten choices ... 40 leaders. Remember, these were not ordinary people, these were **leaders**.

So what would you guess?

How many of these leaders were sponsored in each category?

Do you think more were introduced to network marketing by advertising? More by relatives and friends? More by the Internet and email?

I am going to ask you to think about this for a moment.

... Pause and think.

Decide what you think is the very top category or categories.

So **how** do you think most of the 40 leaders were **introduced** to network marketing?

The answer might surprise you.

And the answer might change how you go about finding new prospects for your business.

And remember, not **ordinary** prospects, but prospects who can become **leaders**.

So . . . are you ready for the answers?

Here are the results:

36 - Relative or friend.

2 - The Internet.

1 - Newspaper advertising.

1 - Radio advertising.

0 - A mailing.

0 - An audio or CD.

0 - At a trade show.

0 - By referral.

0 - By a stranger at a chance encounter.

0 - Saw a flyer.

Amazing, right?

It doesn't take a rocket scientist to see a pattern here. Even in the age of the Internet, only 2 out of 40 leaders were sponsored because of an email campaign, banner ads, a cool web page, etc.

By the way, just so you don't think that I am prejudiced about the results, I was the one leader who was sponsored by newspaper advertising. I answered a newspaper ad back in 1972.

Now, I am not saying that these other methods don't work.

They do work.

But go where the fish are!

Yes, if we want to go fishing, maybe we should go to where the fish are. If 90% (36 out of 40 leaders) are sponsored by a relative or friend, then **why do we spend 90% of our time** trying to find leaders through these other methods?

I know many distributors who try calling cold leads, who buy lists for autoresponders, who run newspaper ads, who try joint ventures with strangers, who pass out flyers and yet they still haven't contacted their warm market of friends.

Crazy, isn't it?

Why not go where the best prospects are **located**?

It's like trying to go shopping by driving down a deserted country road. It makes more sense to go shopping in a shopping mall.

So, if you have some new distributors who are struggling with these cold market techniques, show them this survey.

Show them that they are nine times more likely to find a leader with relatives and friends (their warm market) than all of the other methods **combined**!

But what if I have burned, destroyed and nuked my warm market?

Then the obvious solution is to **first** create a new warm market, and then you will have plenty of warm market prospects again.

Creating a new warm market isn't difficult. You don't have to re-marry to get a new set of in-laws and you don't have to run an ad for friends.

Instead, try some of these ideas:

- Join a club for your favorite hobby.
- Take an evening course at the community college.
- Be nice. Offer to help someone.
- Get involved in a volunteer project.
- Visit garage sales and talk to the browsers.
- Take some time off and go to a party.

- Take the time to visit with clerks, bus drivers, cab drivers, toll booth collectors, and people standing in line.
- Ask people what they like to do in their free time.
- Attend investment and personal finance seminars.

Well, there are plenty more ideas, but we get the point. Just stop trying to look for prospects and start making new friends.

Real friends – not conditional friends!

Make a friend to be a friend. Don't make a conditional friend that you will dump as soon as you realize that he or she is not a prospect.

There are few things uglier than manipulating a person to believe you are a friend, then dumping the person when you realize that you don't have a customer or a distributor.

Just make friends to have friends.

I never hear anyone complaining that they have too many friends. Trust me, it won't be a problem having an extra group of friends.

This same principle applies when you help people. Help people because it is the right thing to do. Don't help people just so you will feel good when they say, "Thank you."

I often hear new distributors say:

"Well, what if I help someone and they don't join my business?"

I often wonder what their parents taught them. Maybe they were taught:

"Don't do anything to help people unless you get paid or get a reward."

If they have that attitude towards helping people, it will eventually show through. You can't hide your beliefs for long. People will find out.

The more friends you have ...

The more friends you have, the easier network marketing becomes. You will have plenty of friends who ask you for solutions to their problems.

Now, they won't all ask on the same day, but over time you will find that your products and business opportunity can help solve some problems for your friends. Pretty easy, isn't it?

Which is the better potential leader?

Imagine that I gave you a choice of two people you could sponsor. Which one would you sponsor?

A. The person with a large network of friends.

B. The person with no warm market but who had the resources to run ads and convince strangers to join your business.

Tough choice? Not for me.

I would choose the person with a large network of friends. This person has a natural market that he can comfortably tap into at no cost. And everyone will give him a favorable hearing.

But it gets better.

Think of his friends. Friends **associate** with people of similar values. This means that his friends will also have a natural network of friends that they can tap into at no cost. And they will be welcomed to give presentations also.

Think about the person with no warm market who only sponsors strangers from advertising. There is no guarantee that these strangers have a large network of friends. **Duplication** could quickly stop with these new distributors.

Person #2 has another problem. He runs an ad. People join. They think that the best way to build their business is by running an ad. After all, that is how they were sponsored.

And do these new people have the skills to run ads? I don't think so. And they fail.

This is the **problem** with buying leads, Internet sponsoring, and most cold methods of sponsoring. These methods require better **skills** to get a presentation or sale. New distributors usually don't have these skills.

But I want to grow fast and I need to use cold market techniques.

Okay. If you must use cold market methods, let's use the same logic. Let's use the methods that have the best chance of succeeding.

I once read an article by a noted sales trainer. In the article, he stated that certain methods had a better chance of success with getting an appointment with a prospect. Here are his results:

- Direct mail .5%
- Cold call 1%
- Two-step 3%
- Referral 15%
- Endorsement 50%

Look at these numbers again.

It took 200 direct mail letters to get one appointment.

It took 100 cold calls to get one appointment.

It took 33 follow-ups to an inquiry (two-step) to get one appointment.

It took 7 referrals to get one appointment.

It took only 2 endorsements to get one appointment.

So which method would be the fastest method to build your business?

Of course you would use endorsements. That would be the best use of your time. If you could get several people to endorse you and your business to their friends, you would be swamped with appointments. That is how to grow fast.

So what's the bottom line?

- Go where the **best** prospects are (warm market.)
- Use the best techniques to get the most appointments (sponsoring skills.)
- Just use common sense.

The best prospect in the world would be someone you saved from a burning building and financed through medical school. You probably don't have a lot of these prospects.

So, go to the next best prospects, your friends.

When you run out of friends, make more friends.

If you decide to work the cold market, at least select a method that gives you the least rejection and the most appointments.

And remember, the key to building a large, successful, and influential network marketing business is to build ... leaders.

FREE!

Get 7 mini-reports of amazing, easy sentences that create new, hot prospects.

Discover how just a few correct words can change your network marketing results forever.

Get all seven free Big Al mini-reports, and the free weekly Big Al Report with more recruiting and prospecting tips.

Sign up today at:

http://www.BigAlReport.com

Want Big Al to speak in your area?

Request a Big Al training event:

http://www.BigAlSeminars.com

Books by Tom "Big Al" Schreiter are available at:

http://www.BigAlBooks.com

See a full line of Big Al products at:

http://www.FortuneNow.com

ABOUT THE AUTHOR

Tom "Big Al" Schreiter has 40+ years of experience in network marketing and MLM. As the author of the original "Big Al" training books in the late '70s, he has continued to speak in over 80 countries on using the exact words and phrases to get prospects to open up their minds and say "YES."

His passion is marketing ideas, marketing campaigns, and how to speak to the subconscious mind in simplified, practical ways. He is always looking for case studies of incredible marketing campaigns that give usable lessons.

As the author of numerous audio trainings, Tom is a favorite speaker at company conventions and regional events.

His blog, **http://www.BigAlBlog.com** is a regular update of network marketing and MLM business-building ideas.

Anyone can subscribe to his free weekly tips at:

http://www.BigAlReport.com

Made in the USA
Lexington, KY
22 June 2018